History of Prussia

A Captivating Guide to the Kingdom of Prussia and Its Role in the Napoleonic Wars, Franco-Prussian War, and Unification of Germany in 1871

© Copyright 2021

All Rights Reserved. No part of this book may be reproduced in any form without permission in writing from the author. Reviewers may quote brief passages in reviews.

Disclaimer: No part of this publication may be reproduced or transmitted in any form or by any means, mechanical or electronic, including photocopying or recording, or by any information storage and retrieval system, or transmitted by email without permission in writing from the publisher.

While all attempts have been made to verify the information provided in this publication, neither the author nor the publisher assumes any responsibility for errors, omissions or contrary interpretations of the subject matter herein.

This book is for entertainment purposes only. The views expressed are those of the author alone, and should not be taken as expert instruction or commands. The reader is responsible for his or her own actions.

Adherence to all applicable laws and regulations, including international, federal, state and local laws governing professional licensing, business practices, advertising and all other aspects of doing business in the US, Canada, UK or any other jurisdiction is the sole responsibility of the purchaser or reader.

Neither the author nor the publisher assumes any responsibility or liability whatsoever on the behalf of the purchaser or reader of these materials. Any perceived slight of any individual or organization is purely unintentional.

Free Bonus from Captivating History (Available for a Limited time)

Hi History Lovers!

Now you have a chance to join our exclusive history list so you can get your first history ebook for free as well as discounts and a potential to get more history books for free! Simply visit the link below to join.

Captivatinghistory.com/ebook

Also, make sure to follow us on Facebook, Twitter and Youtube by searching for Captivating History.

Contents

INTRODUCTION 1
CHAPTER 1 – HUMBLE ORIGINS 3
CHAPTER 2 – RISING FROM THE ASHES 18
CHAPTER 3 – CLIMBING UP THE LADDER 33
CHAPTER 4 – CHANGING SOCIETY 47
CHAPTER 5 – PRIDE AND GLORY 61
CHAPTER 6 – FROM GLORY TO HUMILIATION 74
CHAPTER 7 – RECUPERATION THROUGH REFORMS 92
CHAPTER 8 – EXPANDING DOMINION OVER THE GERMANIC WORLD 107
CHAPTER 9 – FINAL EVOLUTION INTO THE GERMAN EMPIRE 122
EPILOGUE 136
CONCLUSION 138
HERE'S ANOTHER BOOK BY CAPTIVATING HISTORY THAT YOU MIGHT LIKE 140
FREE BONUS FROM CAPTIVATING HISTORY (AVAILABLE FOR A LIMITED TIME) 141
BIBLIOGRAPHY 142

Introduction

Prussia's story, from its inception to its glorious victory through the unification of Germany, is one of an underdog rising to greatness. Over the centuries, the Hohenzollern dynasty led its people and lands, navigating through an obstacle course it seemed destined to fail. Yet, somehow, the Hohenzollerns managed to overcome it, standing atop many other competitors. As such, it can be seen almost as a fairytale or a motivational moral fable. In part, it is exactly that, as Prussia's story follows the classic tale of a small guy who makes it in the world (or, in this case, a small country in a mishmash of medieval German states to a nation-building European power in the late 19th century).

However, at the same time, Prussian history is one marked by militarism, expansionism, and nationalism. Such a portrayal depicts the Prussians as warmongers or a nation of vicious soldiers lacking any scruples. It is seen as a land of "iron and blood." That representation has the same weight and truth to it as the previous, more heroic image. The two are different sides of the same coin, depending solely on our perspective.

This guide will attempt to avoid any judgment of Prussia, regardless of its positive or negative aspects. It will merely retell its story, as it is one that made a substantial mark on European and world history, making it worthy of our attention. It also represents an insight into both German history and culture, as many things that are seen as "quintessentially German" had their roots in Prussia. As such, understanding modern Germany has to be done through the prism of its Prussian ancestors, as they played a key role in the evolution and development of both the German nation and state.

In the end, the Prussian story is one of highs and lows, a meandering tale spanning a long period, showcasing the complexity of the human past. There are wars with victories and losses. There are economic developments and industrialization, educational and religious reforms, diplomacy, trade, and much more. This guide will try to bring you closer to understanding Prussia, Germany, and the history of humankind in general.

Chapter 1 – Humble Origins

Most books concerning Prussian history tend to begin in the 17th century, ignoring centuries of events that helped shaped the development of what was to become the Kingdom of Prussia. With that in mind, this guide will track as far back as possible to set a reference frame in hopes of better understanding the Prussian story.

First, it is important to understand that three components built the Prussian state. The first two are the territories of Brandenburg and Prussia, while the third and most vital is the Hohenzollern dynasty. It emerged from the obscurity of the Middle Ages in the 11th century, with sources mentioning **Burkhard I, Count of Zollern**, who was the ruler of an estate located in the Swabian Alps. It's most likely that the dynasty got its name from this early title, as in those early days, its members were known only as Zollern. Another possibility is that the name was derived from the castle that was the center of their county rule, but in the end, its name remains somewhat uncertain. Similarly, it is quite likely that Burkhard's ancestors were also part of the nobility, although no credible links or sources confirm that. Thus, he remains crowned as the dynasty's founder.

Later paintings of the first Hohenzollern rulers: Burkhard I (top) and Friedrich I (bottom). Source: https://commons.wikimedia.org

Burkhard's successors slowly increased their possessions, mostly by being loyal subjects of the Holy Roman emperors, yet they remained relatively of low prominence and importance. The first step toward a greater fate was made by Friedrich (Frederick) III, who married the heiress of the Burgraviate of Nuremberg. By 1191, he inherited the territory through his wife and became known as Friedrich I, Burgrave of Nuremberg, as this territory was deemed more reputable and richer due to its developed trade.

It seems that at roughly this time, he renamed his dynasty into the Hohenzollerns, roughly translated as the greater Zollerns, most likely to mark its rise in importance. Upon his death, most likely around 1204, his sons, Conrad and Friedrich, divided the inheritance in half. Since Conrad was older, he was given Zollern, while Friedrich received Nuremberg. However, around 1218, for some unknown reason, the two brothers reshuffled the inheritance and switched titles. With that, the House of Hohenzollern was divided into two branches. The younger Friedrich's branch became known as Swabian, while the older Conrad's line became known as Franconian since Nuremberg was located in the region of Franconia, modern-day northwestern Bavaria.

For the next roughly two hundred years, Conrad and his successors remained rather loyal and dependable allies of the Holy Roman Empire. During that period, through clever politics, they managed to slightly enlarge their possessions around Nuremberg, while the city itself became an unofficial capital of the empire where the Imperial Diet would meet from time to time. However, it was only in the early 15th century that the Hohenzollerns made their next step toward prominence. Around 1410, Frederick (Friedrich) VI gained control of the Margravate of Brandenburg, located in northeastern Germany around the city of Berlin. After initial troubles with subduing the local nobles, Frederick consolidated his control. Then, around 1415, he was officially recognized as its legitimate ruler when he paid 400,000 gold pieces to King Sigismund of Hungary, who legally owned the title. Thus, he became known as Frederick I, Margrave of Brandenburg, a title hierarchically between a count and a duke.

The lands themselves were relatively unimposing and worthless. Despite being located in the Central European Plain, its soil wasn't very suitable for agriculture, as it was often sandy and of poor quality. It was also filled with marshes and bogs. Brandenburg also lacked any notable mineral or metal deposits. It was linked with the Baltic coast through the Oder and Elbe Rivers, but those were somewhat sluggish and not interconnected waterways. Furthermore, as the area had little to offer trade-wise, a connection to the sea meant little. Additionally, Brandenburg lacked any natural borders, meaning it was open for invasions.

Overall, the region was utterly unimpressive in terms of its material worth. Its true potential lay in its political importance, as the margrave of Brandenburg was one of seven electoral princes of the Holy Roman Empire. Their official task was to designate the next emperor when needed, and as such, it was a rather distinguished title to hold. Thus, Frederick was also known as the elector of Brandenburg (the prince-elector was a separate title from margrave).

*A 15th-century portrait of Frederick I, Elector of Brandenburg.
Source: https://commons.wikimedia.org*

To understand both the importance of such a distinction and the rest of Hohenzollern and Prussian history, one has to know how the Holy Roman Empire functioned. Unlike most other empires, this wasn't as centralized and unified. It was more akin to a loose federation of some three hundred smaller sovereign territorial entities, whose legal relations and status within the empire varied. Furthermore, the imperial title was elective, making its acquisition a proper game of political intrigue. It is also important to note that despite the existence of an Imperial Diet, there wasn't an imperial central government, the right of taxation, or a standing imperial army. Thus, actual imperial power was somewhat limited. Oftentimes, the strength of the ruler depended solely on his personal possessions, skills, connections, and politics, enabling him to gather or force the support of his numerous subjects. Nevertheless, theoretically, the title was still quite prestigious since the Holy Roman Empire was deemed to be the successor of the Roman Empire. In that political landscape, being one of the prince-electors meant having much more influence and a useful diplomatic tool, allowing for trading votes for other types of concessions like territorial gains.

The Hohenzollerns managed to use their newly acquired influence to secure small but important territorial gains throughout the rest of the 15th and early 16th centuries. They traded their support and votes, but despite that, the dynasty remained relatively weak economically and militarily. At roughly the same time, the famous Habsburg dynasty, whose center of power was in Austria, rose up to dominate the Holy Roman Empire. After decades of political instability, in 1452, Habsburgian Frederick III became the emperor. By then, his dynasty held substantial territories across Europe, allowing him and his successors to dominate relatively small imperial states and entities. Thus, from then on, the imperial title factually became hereditary within the Habsburg line, but it officially and theoretically remained elective. The Habsburgs also began reforming the empire, though they never succeeded in centralizing their rule over those lands as they had in their other possessions like Hungary or Bohemia. Additionally, from 1512, the empire was officially named the Holy Roman Empire of the German Nation, despite having subjects of various other ethnicities. Some see this as the birth of an overarching German national identity, though it was still far from how we perceive such things today.

For the Hohenzollerns, this period was also a time of dynastic consolidation. Up to the late 15th century, the family followed a rather common medieval succession tradition of partitioning the estate between brothers. Such a practice allowed for the suitable security of all the ruler's children, which was rooted in the common familial need to take care of one's offspring. However, it was quite counterproductive from a state-building perspective. This led Albert (Albrecht) III Achilles, who succeeded the margravate from his older brother, to pass the Dispositio Achillea in 1473, a law stipulating that Brandenburg must remain whole and could only be solely inherited by his eldest son. However, the rest of the Nurembergian lands remained dividable.

This was the first Hohenzollern succession law, yet it initially was meant to regulate only the matter of Albert's heirs. This notion of an indivisible Brandenburgian estate was confirmed once again in 1541 with the House Treaty of Regensburg, which concerned the redistribution of Nuremberg territories among the later Hohenzollerns. Along the way, there were attempts and even short-term divisions of Brandenburg; however, by the late 16th century, the idea of its unitary nature prevailed among the dynasty, signaling the transformation from clan chiefs into heads of states.

Despite that, the turn of the century proved to be turbulent for the Hohenzollerns, as well as the entire Holy Roman Empire. In 1517, Martin Luther's *Nighty-five Theses* sparked the start of the religious Reformation that formalized the split of Catholics and Protestants. This caused shockwaves across Europe and created numerous religious conflicts, but it proved particularly harmful for the empire's peace. Many of the northern Germanic states turned toward Protestantism, most notably Lutheranism. For the Catholic south, that was heresy, especially for the deeply devoted Habsburgs, who often saw themselves as the bulwarks of Christianity due to the long-lasting clashes with the Ottoman Turks in the Balkans. As such, Emperor Charles V of House Habsburg saw fit to fight against the Lutheran north, also using it to consolidate his imperial rule. With that, the Hohenzollerns found themselves in the midst of the ensuing chaos.

The Swabian line remained Catholic, as did most of the southern Germanic states. However, Brandenburg was heavily influenced by the new religion. When Lutheranism emerged, Prince-elector Joachim I acted like a devoted Catholic, trying to repress it. This was partially because he substantially profited from the selling of indulgences (Martin Luther's biggest issue with the corrupt Catholic Church), which was done by his own brother Albert, who was the archbishop of Magdeburg. In fact, Albert was one of the clerical leaders that sparked Luther's rebellion and one of the people directly accused in the *Nighty-five Theses*. However, his wife, Elizabeth of Denmark, publicly converted to Lutheranism, sparking a split between them.

Along with that, the Brandenburgian commoners began turning toward the new Christian branch, prompting Joachim to force his son and heir Joachim II to sign a contract promising to remain a Catholic. Joachim II honored the agreement but only for a while. By 1539, four years after his father's death and his own ascension to the throne, he converted to Lutheranism. Nevertheless, he refused to force his subjects to follow him while also avoiding any public support for his new religion. Joachim II was worried, quite rightfully, that any excess in such matters might put him and Brandenburg in danger, as the empire was still overwhelmingly Catholic.

Thus, politically, he remained a loyal subject of the Habsburgian emperor. Joachim II even sent a small contingent of troops to aid the emperor in the Schmalkaldic War (1546-1547), a religious conflict with German Lutheran princes. In most cases, Joachim II tried to separate himself from most of the radical and belligerent Lutheran leaders while also refusing to abandon his beliefs. Instead, he tried to secure peace for his realm by attempting to act as a mediator between the two sides. The situation subsided a bit in the 1550s when Holy Roman Emperor Charles V agreed to negotiate with the Protestants. He was partially forced to do this since France began to aid the rebellious princes, seeking to destabilize his reign. This led to the Peace of Augsburg of 1555, which allowed both Lutheranism and Catholicism under the principle of "whose realm, his religion." This meant that rulers were allowed to choose confessions of their own estates. It's worth mentioning that other branches of Protestantism weren't allowed by this agreement. Regardless, this allowed Joachim II to publicly endorse Lutheranism in 1563 when the situation had calmed down.

Thus, the Margravate of Brandenburg slowly went through a religious transformation throughout the 16th century. The process picked up speed in the century's last decades when Joachim's successors began reinforcing Lutheranism more avidly. Nevertheless, even then, they refrained from overly antagonizing other Catholic princes, remaining loyal to the Habsburg emperors. The Hohenzollerns knew that the Augsburg agreement gave them only relative security. Despite being in a somewhat difficult position, as they were unable to expand their territory through wars or transactions to gain more strength, the margraves of Brandenburg were still ambitious. Continuing the proven method of their ancestors, the Hohenzollern princes relied on marriage to achieve that. Initially, it seemed these attempts were futile. No major gains were achieved during the 16th century, as marriages with the ruling families of Denmark and Pomerania failed to grant the Hohenzollerns much-needed Baltic harbors. However, Joachim II did manage to create a foundation of a crucial expansion that would forever change the fate of the dynasty.

A portrait of Joachim II. Source: https://commons.wikimedia.org

In 1535, Joachim II married Princess Hedwig of Poland, which was a rather powerful state at the time. More importantly, King Sigismund I of Poland was a feudal lord of a Baltic duchy that caught Joachim's eye. The Duchy of Prussia was the third component of the Prussian state, and this Prussian territory would be the one to later lend its name to the entire country. The duchy was located on the Baltic coast, around the modern-day city of Kaliningrad. It's worth noting that Ducal Prussia constituted only the eastern half of the historical Prussian territory, as its western parts around present-day Gdansk were fully integrated into the Polish crown, being known as Royal Prussia. Regardless, the Duchy of Prussia was more than a worthy prize for Brandenburg. Not only would it gain important Baltic harbors but also fertile lands suitable for wheat farming. Besides these valuable features, the duchy also caught Joachim's eyes due to the fact that it was ruled by his cousin from the Hohenzollern side branch, Duke Albert of Prussia.

Albert, the grandson of Albert III Achilles, came to hold that title more by luck than design. As a member of a side branch and a third son, he was poised for a clerical career. He was a devout Catholic and seemed to be a reliable and learned man. Thus, when the Teutonic Order needed a new grandmaster, he was elected for the role in 1511. At the time, the order held Prussia, as it had been present there since the early 13th-century Prussian crusade sought to Christianize the local population. After their goal was achieved, the knights stayed, becoming a rival for surrounding states, most notably Poland and Lithuania. From the mid-15th century, the Teutonic Order saved itself from destruction by accepting suzerainty from Polish kings, becoming a Polish fiefdom. Nevertheless, relations remained strained. In fact, part of the reason why Albert was chosen was due to the fact his mother hailed from the Polish ruling family, making him the king's nephew. Despite his attempts to salvage the situation, he found affairs in Prussia slipping out of his hands. That was when he met with Martin Luther, who persuaded him to adopt Lutheranism and convert Prussia to his personal estate.

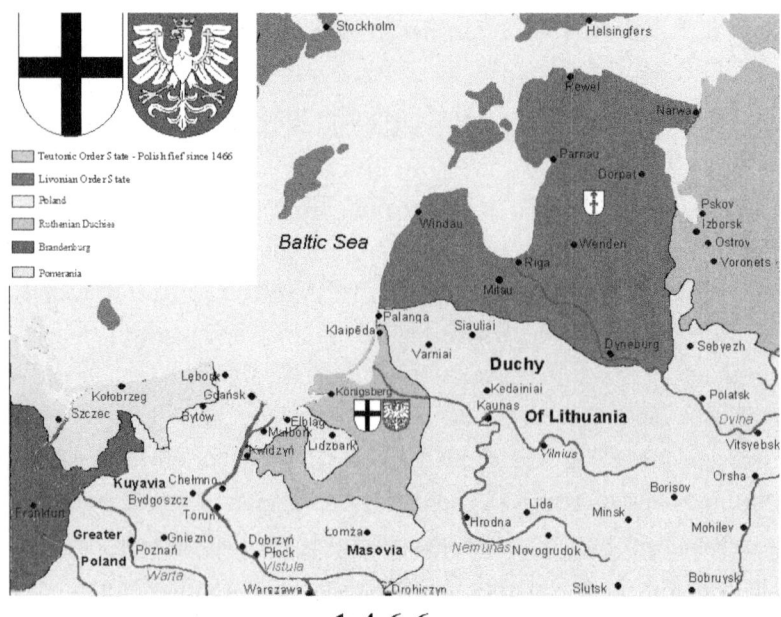

A map of Prussia under the Teutonic Knights (in orange).
Source: https://commons.wikimedia.org

Using his ties with the Polish king, Albert managed to secure that. Thus, in 1525, the Duchy of Prussia was formally established, remaining a Polish fiefdom. Simultaneously, Prussia and Albert became among the earliest public supporters of Lutheranism. However, years passed, and as he was nearing the end of his life, he left only a single male heir, Albert Frederick, who was underaged. This prompted Joachim II to act, and in 1564, he used his wife's connections to secure a decree deeming his sons as secondary heirs to the duchy if Albert Frederick died without an heir. This was confirmed four years later when the old duke died.

It was a long-term plan that eventually paid off. Though Albert Frederick lived a long life, dying only in 1618, he left no heirs, as he was mentally ill. However, even before his death, the Brandenburgian Hohenzollerns acted to secure their succession. Joachim's grandson, Joachim Frederick, persuaded the Polish king to give him regency over the mentally unstable Albert in 1603. He also arranged a marriage between his son John (Johann) Sigismund and Albert's daughter, Anna of Prussia, in 1594, disregarding candid warnings from her mother that the duchess wasn't the easiest on the eyes.

As if that wasn't enough, Joachim Frederick went on to marry Anna's younger sister, becoming his son's brother-in-law. Such actions only showcase how contrived and convoluted political marriages were between the nobles of that era. An additional layer of marital and succession complexity came from Anna's female lineage. Her mother was part of the Jülich-Cleves family, which had its own inheritance law that allowed female members to receive titles if there were no other heirs. Thus, because Anna's uncle, who was mentally ill like her father, had no direct heirs, she was next in line to inherit the Jülich-Cleves lands located near the German-Dutch border, around the Rhine River. Of course, Anna's inheritance was far from sure, both for Prussia and for the Jülich-Cleves territories.

First of all, Anna and John weren't the only claimants, and even more troublesome was the fact that neither of the territories adjoined with Brandenburg. Finally, acquiring and holding them required the prince-elector to have the support of his Brandenburgian elites, whose interests were local and had no interest in far-away lands. Trying to compensate for that, in 1605, Joachim Frederick allied himself with the prince-elector of Palatinate, an important noble in the Rhine region. Joachim betrothed his grandson, Georg Wilhelm, to his daughter, which allowed him to become connected with the Dutch, who was a long-time enemy of the Habsburgs, fighting against them since 1560. Furthermore, Palatinate was the center of Calvinism, a more radical form of Protestantism. For the first time, the Hohenzollerns swayed from neutrality and loyalty to the emperor, aligning themselves with the Habsburgs' enemies.

Brandenburg's position soon worsened; in 1608, Joachim Frederick passed away, leaving John to battle for the inheritance of the Jülich-Cleves territories the following year. The religious turbulence of the period led to a clash between the Catholic League and the

Protestant Union about the issue, two religion-based alliances of Germanic states. The conflict quickly escalated as the Habsburgs, Dutch, French, and English got involved. In the ensuing chaos, the margrave of Brandenburg was just slightly more than an observer, as his power and wealth were far from competitive with the other major actors. However, John Sigismund himself began further complicating his position in those turbulent times. In 1613, he announced his conversion to Calvinism, a religion that wasn't recognized by the Peace of Augsburg of 1555, leaving him exposed even more. Then, making matters worse, the Protestant Union withdrew its support for his claims in 1617, prompting him to leave the union. In a whirlwind of religious and political struggles, Brandenburg stood alone.

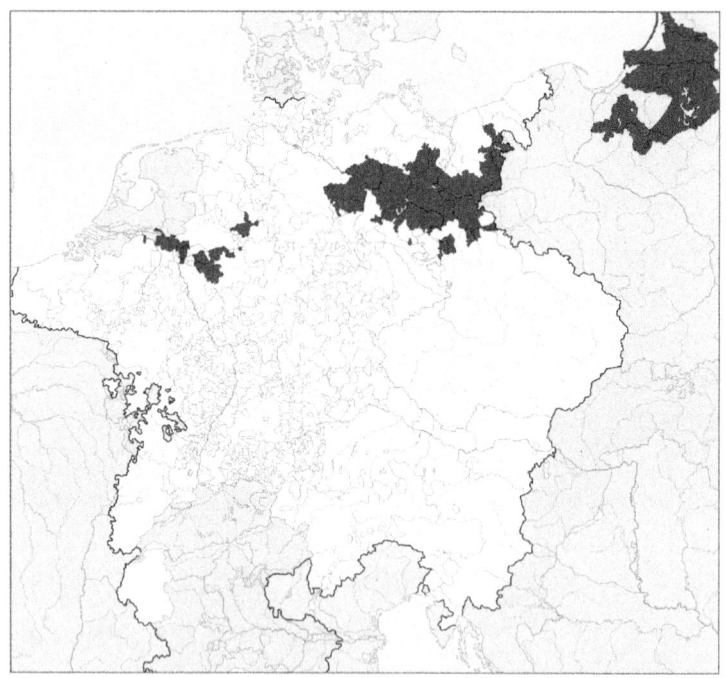

A map showing Brandenburg-Prussia within the Holy Roman Empire in 1618. Source: https://commons.wikimedia.org

As if that wasn't enough trouble for the Hohenzollerns, John's health was quickly declining from his abuse of alcohol and very possibly the stresses caused by the events. He became erratic, obese, and lethargic. Then, in 1616, he suffered a stroke, leaving his speech impaired. It seemed uncertain if he would live long enough to inherit Prussia. Yet, with some luck for his heirs, Duke Albert Frederick died in 1618, activating another claim for John. However, John Sigismund quickly passed it to his son, Georg Wilhelm, as he died in 1619. Prussia and Brandenburg then entered into a personal union under Georg's rule, creating the first outlines of a state that would become known as Prussia, one of Europe's leading powers in later centuries. Nonetheless, at that moment, the future of Brandenburg-Prussia and the Hohenzollerns seemed far from certain, as the Holy Roman Empire and large chunks of Europe got involved in the Thirty Years' War (1618-1648).

Chapter 2 – Rising from the Ashes

Just as the Brandenburg-Prussian union was coming to fruition after almost a century of careful planning by several generations of the Hohenzollern dynasty, a storm appeared above the Holy Roman Empire. With the rising competition between the Catholics and the Protestants, the empire slowly descended into conflict, which grew from a religious confrontation into a power struggle between the major European powers. Unfortunately for the Hohenzollerns, Brandenburg was caught up in the middle of it.

The war began in 1618, just as Albert Frederick passed away, leaving Brandenburg with two unsolved claims. Its inception was when Protestant Bohemia (the modern-day Czech Republic) rose up against the Catholic Habsburg rule, trying to install a Calvinist king on the throne. The war quickly spread across the Holy Roman Empire, as local princes, dukes, and counts swore fealty to either side.

Amidst the chaos, Prince-elector Georg Wilhelm tried to return the Hohenzollerns to neutrality. He avoided fully committing himself to any alliance or side, often relying solely on moral support or empty promises. However, such neutrality could only be upheld with military backing, something none of the Hohenzollern estates provided. In the anarchic and violent clashes of the Thirty Years' War, an unspoken rule was "either you're with us or against us." Thus, Georg Wilhelm's attempts at impartiality left him more or less against everyone.

First, in 1623, a part of the Jülich-Cleves territories that were under Georg's control was invaded by the Protestant League, despite his supposed neutrality. Then, three years later, as he was trying to raise some money to gather at least some troops, parts of Brandenburg were invaded by the Danes, who entered the war on the Protestant side. Despite sharing the same religious beliefs, Brandenburg suffered heavy looting. Soon afterward, imperial troops entered Brandenburg, forcing the margrave to swear fealty to the emperor. Yet, the looting continued, just at the hand of a different army. Simultaneously, the Duchy of Prussia was invaded by Sweden, which used it as a base against Poland. Making matters even more complicated, Georg's sister was married to King Gustavus Adolphus of Sweden. Their connection became even more troubling for the prince-elector around 1630 when Sweden became involved with the Holy Roman Empire's war.

Georg Wilhelm once again tried to return to neutrality, yet the Swedish army marched toward Berlin. Gustavus Adolphus forced Georg into an alliance by giving him an ultimatum. Besides that, the imperial massacre of the Protestant city of Magdeburg in 1631 also helped the margrave to decide. In the summer of that year, Brandenburg-Prussia became a Swedish ally, giving Sweden monetary tribute and the right to its lands for military purposes. In return, the prince-elector was promised parts of Pomerania, a region on the Baltic coast between the Recknitz and Vistula Rivers.

However, the initial Swedish supremacy was cut down by Gustavus's death in 1632, and by 1635, the Habsburgs were once again a winning party. This led Georg Wilhelm to switch sides once again. In return, the emperor promised to honor the claim on Pomerania. Nevertheless, the Swedes were still a force to be reckoned with, and in 1636, they returned to Brandenburg as the enemy, which was ravaged by both the Swedish and imperial armies. Unable to fend for himself, Georg Wilhelm fled to the Duchy of Prussia, where he hid until his death in 1640.

Later generations of the Hohenzollern rulers deemed Georg Wilhelm to be a bad and indecisive ruler, ascertaining that if he had been succeeded by another ruler like him, both the dynasty and Brandenburg would have been lost to obscurity. Parts of these claims are based on the fact that Brandenburg-Prussia was at its lowest point under Georg's reign. It suffered unimaginable destruction and death. Its population was ravaged, in some regions losing more than 50 percent of its populace. In extreme cases, some smaller towns were completely abandoned. People were starving and dying, suffering atrocities from numerous conquerors and plagued by illnesses and disease. Brandenburg's modest economy was also on the brink, with certain areas losing up to 50 to 60 percent of their farms to destruction and desertion. However, considering the tough position in which Georg Wilhelm was put in, it is questionable how much better a more capable leader could have actually done.

Georg Wilhelm (top) and his son Frederick William, the Great Elector (bottom). Source: https://commons.wikimedia.org

Brandenburg was surrounded by hostile states that were seeking solely to exploit it, and Brandenburg had little capability to fend for itself. This was partially caused by Georg's timid and indecisive nature, which had been caused by a wound from a hunting accident in his youth. However, his choices were, in reality, always between two evils, making his hesitations more than reasonable. Furthermore, he faced substantial opposition from within. His own aristocratic subjects often refused to aid him in money, troops, and other resources, showing little care for Brandenburg's survival. Part of their disagreement came from the fact they were mostly Lutheran while the elector was a Calvinist. Initial disagreements became less important as the war and occupation crushed what little administration existed before it. The margrave's position was only more impaired by the actions and stances of the women of his court, whose religious beliefs narrowed his diplomatic scope. His wife was a passionate Calvinist, while his mother was a devoted Lutheran, both of whom used their personal and familial connections to steer the Hohenzollerns against the Catholic Habsburgs. Thus, when assessing Georg Wilhelm's rule, all of these aggravating circumstances only emphasized his faults. Had he ruled in more peaceful times, he may have been a decent enough ruler. Nonetheless, fate pushed him into a chaos that few could navigate successfully.

Luckily for the Hohenzollerns, his son and heir proved to be a more than capable successor. Frederick William (Friedrich Wilhelm) ascended to the throne in 1640 at the age of twenty, having been shielded from all the death and destruction for most of his childhood. His earliest days were spent in a secure fortress, focused on learning. Then, at the age of fourteen, he was sent to some relatives in the Dutch Republic, which was going through its golden age of naval and economic supremacy. Frederick William's time there seemed to have influenced him the most, as he strived to emulate its success. He wanted to impose the rule of law and impose the state as the guarantee of order, along with a robust financial system that could support the government. Throughout his reign, the prince-elector continuously tried to base Brandenburg's economy on maritime trade as the Dutch did for themselves. Finally, while in the Dutch Republic, he had seen that the republic had well-trained and well-organized troops, which he realized was needed if there was to be peace and stability for Brandenburg-Prussia.

However, all these ideas would have fallen flat if it was not for two important distinctions between Frederick William and his predecessors. One was a sharp mind, trained by years of schooling and learning. The other, probably the most important, was his diligence. He saw his role as the prince-elector not merely as a prestigious title aligned with a bundle of rights and revenues and packed in a bale of ceremonies and formalities. Instead, Frederick William thought of it as his job, a vocation that required all his time and effort. Thus, he worked hard on fulfilling his duties and responsibilities. Arguably, his success stemmed from this more than any other quality he may have had. Nevertheless, his early years on the throne proved the most difficult, especially as the young Frederick William had no actual experience in governing and had to contend with the Thirty Years' War on top of that.

The young prince-elector remained "confined" to his Prussian estate for the first three years of the rule, returning to Brandenburg for the first time in years in 1643. There, he found destruction and misery, as various stragglers and bandits continued to plague the lands even after the Swedish retreated around 1642. In those early years of his reign, Frederick focused on enlarging his army, managing to expand it from a measly three thousand men in 1642 to about eight thousand around 1645. Though still small compared to other forces, it was a considerable increase for Brandenburg-Prussia. A strong army was also vital if the state was to survive, as the prince-elector and his advisors feared that the Polish would seize Prussia as soon as possible. In addition, the Swedes were still present in Pomerania, while relations with the Habsburgs were still rocky. Even the westernmost Cleves was under threat from the Dutch and French. Luckily for the

Hohenzollerns, by the 1640s, most of Europe was tired of what seemed to be an unending war. After years of preparations and then negotiations, the Peace of Westphalia was signed in 1648, ending the prolonged conflict.

The main negotiators for the peace were the Habsburgs, both the Austrian and Spanish branches; France, which entered the war at a later stage; Sweden; Denmark; and the Dutch Republic, along with dozens of smaller state representatives, like the one hailing from Berlin. Those delegations had little sway over matters, but thankfully for Frederick William, France decided to back his claims in an attempt to curb Habsburg power. As such, delegates from Paris agreed with their Swedish allies that the prince-elector would gain eastern parts of Pomerania, honoring, in part, previous agreements with Frederick's father. Then, the two allies pressed the Holy Roman emperor to grant the margrave the former bishoprics of Magdeburg, Halberstadt, Kammin, and Minden as compensation for losing western Pomerania to Sweden. The treaty also confirmed the Hohenzollern rule over the Cleves part of the Jülich-Cleves territories. These acquisitions proved to be vital for the development of Brandenburg-Prussia, as they closed the gap between the central provinces while also making Brandenburg-Prussia the second-largest state of the Holy Roman Empire after the Habsburg estate.

After the war ended, the prince-elector continued his work on establishing a more substantial standing army. He modernized its armaments by introducing lighter and faster firing flintlocks and standardized artillery calibers while also prompting his paid troops to go through constant training and exercise. In establishing a cadet school, Frederick created a constant and stable officer cadre, as well as a standardized professional army formation. All of these military reforms had come from the successful practices of the French, Dutch, Swedes, and even the imperial army. The crowning achievement was the 1655 establishment of the general war commissioner (*Generalkriegkommissar*), which was modeled on recent French reforms. The new office was tasked with overseeing the administrative needs of the army. The office of a war commissioner was supposed to be temporary, and its command wasn't spread equally across the Hohenzollern estates. Nevertheless, over the decades, it expanded both in its territorial reach as well as in prerogatives, slowly decreasing the importance of local nobles in military matters. Despite that, the war commissioner remained a relatively small institution, yet it was, in a way, the inception of the famous Prussian General Staff of later times.

The war commissioner's first "temporary" task was to handle the army's needs in the so-called Second Northern War (1655-1660) between Sweden and Poland, as well as their various allies. The conflict was, in essence, Gustavus's heir's attempt to emulate his predecessor by taking more lands from Poland, among them the Duchy of Prussia, which was still legally a Polish fief. In early 1656, Frederick William tried to negotiate his way out of another threat by allying with the Swedes while gaining full sovereignty of the duchy in return. By that time, the military reforms had increased the Brandenburg-Prussian Army to about twenty-five thousand well-trained soldiers. They, together with the prince-elector himself, proved their worth in the Battle of Warsaw in the summer of that year. The joint Swedish-Prussian army, about eighteen thousand strong, managed to defeat the Polish, who had a force over twice as large. The participation of Frederick's soldiers finally convinced the Swedish to give in to his demands for Prussia's sovereignty. However, the war quickly turned, as the Polish got aid from the Habsburgs and Denmark. Now, the prince-elector sought to gain the same concession from the other side.

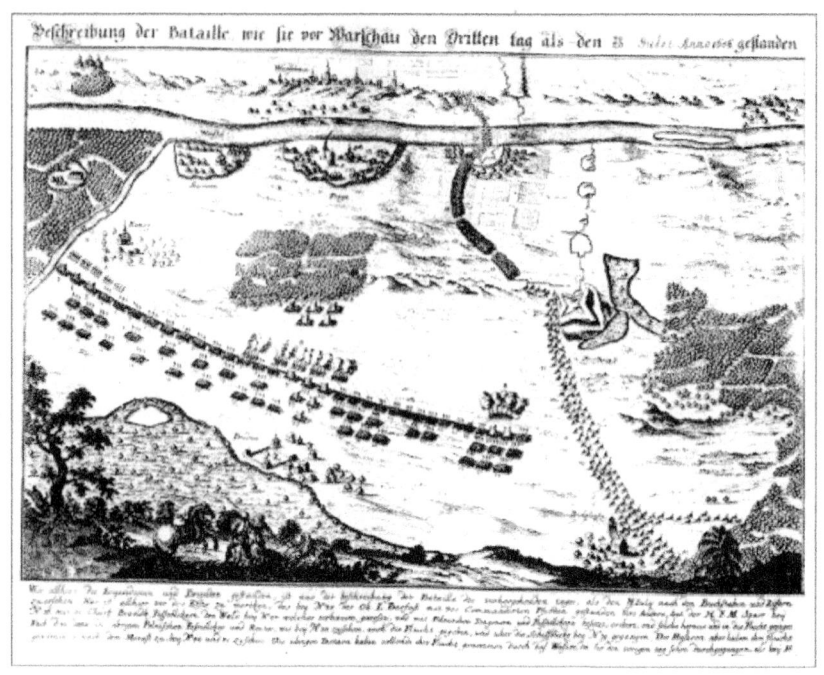

Contemporary illustration of the Battle of Warsaw.
Source: https://commons.wikimedia.org

His military success made him a worthy ally, especially since the Polish king sought to break apart the Swedish-Brandenburg alliance in fear of their connection, as well as the growing threat from Russia. Another important occurrence was the death of the Habsburg emperor in 1657, which allowed the prince-elector to trade his vote for support on the matter. Eventually, joint pressure forced the Polish king to accept Frederick's terms; thus, in September 1657, the Duchy of Prussia became an independent land, with its full sovereignty in Frederick William's hands. In the following two years, he and his army proved their worth some more, playing an important role in ousting the Swedes from the Baltic coast. By 1660, the sides began their negotiations, where the prince-elector hoped to secure the rest of Pomerania for himself. However, his claims were shut down by the French, who claimed that such an event would be in breach of the Peace of Westphalia. France wanted Sweden to maintain its presence in the north, as it would act as a constant threat to France's Habsburg rivals. This taught Frederick William that military strength could only carry him to a certain degree; after all, in the grander European picture, Brandenburg-Prussia was seen as a minor actor.

After such a diplomatic failure, the prince-elector realized that alliances were as important as his armies. Thus, through the 1660s and early 1670s, he utilized Brandenburg-Prussia's position as an important regional partner, switching his allegiances between France and Austria and milking them both for additional monetary subsidies needed for maintaining and further increasing his armies. Then, in 1672, the Franco-Dutch War erupted. With Frederick William's western provinces threatened, he aligned himself with the Habsburg emperor, who instinctively sought to curb French expansion. Nevertheless, the prince-elector maintained contact with Paris, keeping his option open. However, his position was firmly set in December 1674 when the traditional French ally of Sweden invaded Brandenburg, starting the so-called Scanian War. Frederick William rushed back from campaigning in the west, bringing only a fraction of his troops with him. The memory of the Thirty Years' War was still fresh, and he intended to prevent a repeat of that occupation scenario.

The prince-elector, along with roughly six thousand soldiers, arrived home by early summer. Once there, he quickly pounced at the invaders, whose main army numbered roughly eleven thousand men. After some smaller clashes, Frederick William managed to force the Swedes into a major confrontation in the Battle of Fehrbellin. Despite the Swedes' numerical advantage, he managed to outmaneuver them so that they were unable to commit all of their forces to the battle. The Brandenburgians managed to rout the enemy in a single afternoon. The battle itself had minor casualties, roughly five hundred on both sides. However, the Swedes found themselves beset by vengeful peasants and a pursuing army, so they lost many more during the retreat in the following days. Soon, Brandenburg was free of invaders, allowing its prestige to grow. The battle was later characterized as the final breaking point of the mythical "invincible"

Swedish army, while the later Hohenzollerns tended to overplay its importance. They used it to mark the mythical inception of the supposedly unbeatable Prussian military. Even Frederick William realized the propaganda value of such a victory. Utilizing the fact that he personally led the army, he began referring to himself as the "Great Elector." From then on, this battle was seen and represented as the point of Prussian rebirth, as it emerged as an important European power.

However, the reality was far from such grandeur. Over the next couple of years, the Great Elector managed to take control of the entire Swedish Pomerania once again by winning more battles. Yet, when the Franco-Dutch War ended in 1678, the major powers were bent on ending the Scanian War as well. In 1679, France more or less dictated that all territory lost by Sweden during the war should be returned. The Habsburgs agreed, as they, too, were more in favor of having a weak Sweden than a strong Brandenburg. Frederick William's hands were tied, as, even with his roughly 38,000 soldiers, he wasn't a match to the French Army, which had roughly 250,000 men. Despite all his achievements, both the Great Elector and Brandenburg-Prussia were still a second-rate power. Thus, after the war ended, Frederick was forced to return to his "pendulum alliance policy," quickly changing allegiances and searching to extort as much money as he could.

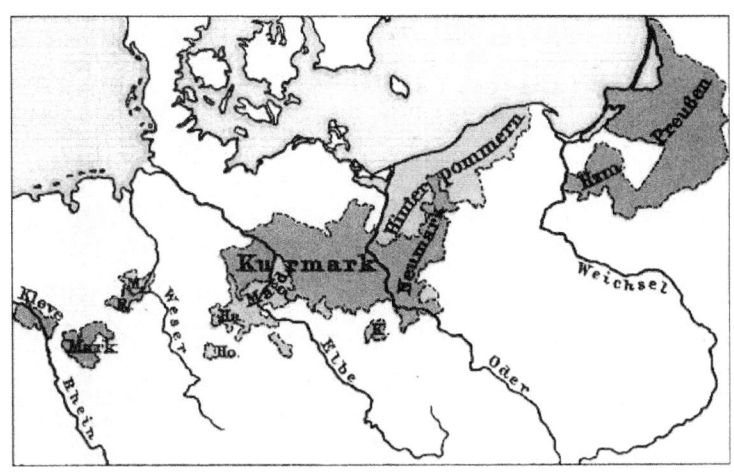

A map depicting Brandenburg-Prussian territory in 1640 (red) and its territorial expansion by 1688 (green). Source: https://commons.wikimedia.org

Looking solely from that viewpoint, it seemed like not much had changed from his father's reign. However, the Great Elector's alliance policy was of his own choice. While Georg Wilhelm was forced by others to switch allegiances, Frederick William did that to benefit himself. Furthermore, under his reign, the economy managed to not only recover but expand to new heights. He used his connection with the Dutch (he was married to a member of the Orange family) to attract artisans, builders, farmers, and traders from the Lowlands, who brought modern technologies and methods with them. Then, in 1685, Frederick opened up his borders for about twenty thousand Huguenots who had fled France in fear of persecution, which also helped with the economic development of the Hohenzollern lands. Furthermore, the Great Elector tried to get Brandenburg involved in the Atlantic "triangular trade" by establishing both the Brandenburg-Prussian navy and the Brandenburg African Company (later renamed the Brandenburg African American Company), which were both modeled after the Dutch, in the 1680s. Despite the failure of maritime and colonial ambitions, during his long reign, Frederick William managed to create an economic basis for the future Prussian state.

Apart from economic development, Frederick also worked on establishing a working state administration. First, he created the position of the Officer of Domains (*Amtskammer*), who was tasked with administering his personal estates. Then, he founded tax commissioners, which, in turn, led to the creation of local administrations headed by a governor who was elected by the regional nobility. Furthermore, Frederick William worked on curbing the power and rights of the nobility by isolating them and pitting them against each other in blind pursuit of their local needs, allowing his power as the head of state to grow. He also incorporated gifted and capable lowborn individuals into the government, as well as in the army, creating the seed for the future Prussian ideal of merit. Nevertheless, in the end, Frederick William's most important and influential achievement was gaining full sovereignty of the Duchy of Prussia, which was to become the cornerstone of the entire Brandenburg-Prussia.

In May of 1688, Frederick William passed away after forty-eight years on the throne, leaving the fate of Brandenburg-Prussia in the hands of his son, now Prince-elector Frederick III. Similar to the previous succession, the new ruler differed greatly from his predecessor. He lacked most of the qualities his father had, something the Great Elector never hid from his son (Frederick William called his son a disappointment). In fact, Frederick William favored his older brother, Charles (Karl) Emil, who showed great talent, charisma, and military aptitude. However, Charles died during the Franco-Dutch War, leaving Frederick next in line for the throne. Unlike his brother, Frederick was sensitive, temperamental, and lacked fighting prowess, mostly due to a childhood injury. Frederick III, who was slightly paranoid, even feared the rest of his family was out to get him in the last years of his father's life, hiding with his in-laws in Hanover. Thanks to this familial disharmony and his clashes with his predecessor, Frederick wasn't properly introduced to state affairs or the hardships of ruling.

As if that wasn't enough, the Great Elector left a testament that ordered the partition of the Hohenzollern lands, as he wished to leave some inheritance for his children from his second marriage. Thus, Frederick's first years on the throne were focused on negating this, calling upon the dynasty succession laws of previous centuries. Only by the early 1690s did he manage to secure his primacy. Nevertheless, the new prince-elector, who was in his thirties, knew exactly what he wanted. He aimed at receiving a kingly title, building upon his father's legacy. His plans hinged upon the fact that Prussia was legally outside of the Holy Roman Empire, as imperial law generally forbade the title of king (the Kingdom of Bohemia was an exception due to its complicated history and ties with the Habsburg dynasty). In the second half of the 1690s, Frederick began various negotiations, trying to find a diplomatic solution to fulfill his goal. Finally, a ripe opportunity arose in late 1700 when the Spanish Habsburg king died without an heir, sparking the War of the Spanish Succession (1701–1714).

A Brandenburgian coin of Frederick I from 1691.
Source: https://commons.wikimedia.org

While Holy Roman Emperor Leopold I of House Habsburg prepared for the war, Frederick asked him for the royal crown of Prussia in return for sending eight thousand soldiers for the conflict. He claimed that since Prussia was never a part of the empire, there was no legal obstacle for him to be crowned. A compromise was made when Leopold agreed that Frederick could become the "king in Prussia." Note the difference in wording; typically, one is the "king of" a certain land. This is an important distinction, as it meant that other lands within the empire weren't raised to this new hierarchical level and that the emperor merely recognized the kingly title instead of creating it. It also played against possible Polish claims, as they still held western "royal" parts of Prussia. Thus, in January 1701, the prince-elector crowned himself, sending a message of his independence from any worldly or clerical authority and becoming known as King Frederick I. This was a departure from most other coronation traditions across Europe. The rest of the ceremony, symbolism, and even the new royal insignia was designed by Frederick himself, who borrowed from older and newer traditions from other courts, all in a design to showcase his new, all-encompassing monarchical power and independence.

Despite the pomp, the wording of the title provided some amusement and bewilderment to the European courts. Nevertheless, with minor exceptions, most of the rulers accepted the title as a valid one. Thus, within less than a century, the Hohenzollerns managed to escape from the brink of destruction and rise to a kingly status, no matter how limited it was.

Chapter 3 – Climbing up the Ladder

Achieving a kingly status proved to be only the first step for the Hohenzollerns. The feeling of shame, helplessness, and desperation carved by the traumas of the Thirty Years' War pushed them beyond mere recognition. Their goal was never to allow such misery to fall upon their lands and people. A title alone wouldn't prevent that, so they continued to work on making their state stronger and capable of fending for itself.

For that reason, many of the later Hohenzollerns passed harsh judgment on King Frederick I. From their perspective, he was a vain ruler, hiding in his ivory tower, focused on empty ceremonies. Some of his successors even claimed he was focused on gaining kingly recognition solely so he could find excuses for the lavish life he dreamed of having. Furthermore, unlike his warrior father, he stayed away from wars and, even worse, "reduced" the Prussian military to mercenaries. As a means of generating additional revenue, he often leased his troops to fight in other wars, which was, in some sense, a disgrace to what was becoming the ideal Prussian leader. However, such accusations of being a failed ruler is unfair propaganda of later times when Prussia already had a forged military identity.

Coronation of Frederick I in Königsberg.
Source: https://commons.wikimedia.org

In reality, Frederick I was a decent ruler whose rule achieved more than just displays of splendor. First of all, during his reign, most of Europe was once again hit with a series of large-scale wars. By staying away from those, Frederick might have lost an opportunity to expand his realm, but he also spared his lands from more devastation. Secondly, unlike his militarily orientated father and later son, he was more of an intellectual. Frederick spoke several languages, and he was interested in the science and arts, with an urban, gregarious, and mild-mannered personality. Thus, instead of building more barracks, he invested in the creation of the Academy of Arts (1696) and Academy of Sciences (1700). Furthermore, during his reign, Berlin began its transformation into a proper European capital. By 1710, Frederick merged it with its suburbs and proclaimed it his capital, all the while decorating it with various ornamental structures, which hid the scars from the Thirty Years' War. The downside of all the aforementioned patronages and investments in decorum and ceremonies was that they were expensive, something for which his heirs never really "forgave" him. Nevertheless, the final verdict his own grandson wrote about him was that Frederick I was great in small matters and small in great matters.

Frederick's rule ended in 1713 when his fragile health finally failed. He was succeeded by his eldest son, King Frederick William (Friedrich Wilhelm) I, who was numbered as the first because his previous namesakes didn't hold the royal title. As the almost polar opposite of his father, Frederick William was, above all, frugal and antisocial, focused on practicality and military matters. The differences between him and Frederick I were clear from his youth, as his unruly behavior drove his teachers mad. One of them even said that he would have been happier as a galley slave than the prince's tutor. Unlike his father, Frederick William spoke only German but barely wrote it. He did possess a sharp intellect, prompting some historians to theorize he suffered from dyslexia, which could also explain, to a degree, his disinterest in the arts. The young king was also rather blunt and distrustful, and he was prone to violent outbursts and melancholic episodes. Yet, despite all their differences, Frederick William had the utmost respect for his father. In turn, Frederick I was determined to introduce his son to matters of state so he wouldn't face the same difficulties he did at the beginning of his reign. Thus, by the age of fourteen, Frederick William had become a part of his father's privy council and, a year later, war council.

The good relations and relative harmony between the two were disrupted in 1709/10 when the plague spread across Prussia, killing more than a third of its population. Twenty-two-year-old Frederick William openly criticized his father for his ineptitude and mismanagement of his ministers. However, instead of an open confrontation between the two, Frederick I backed down and even began transferring power to his son, meaning that the last years of his reign were almost a co-regency. Faced with corruption and the inefficiency of the existing system, Frederick William started expressing his disdain for such behavior and his determination to mend it. Simultaneously, the plague increased his resolve to further strengthen the Brandenburg-Prussian Army while also increasing its independence from foreign subsidies. This feeling came from the fact that the disease was brought by passing Russian and Swedish troops during the Great Northern War (1700-1721), which disregarded Prussian neutrality while its troops were tied up in the War of the Spanish Succession. Thus, the great crisis of his father's reign was the catalyst for Frederick William's two most important legacies: reforms of the military and state administration.

A painting of Frederick William I. Source: https://commons.wikimedia.org

Nevertheless, he respected his father's wishes, giving him a grand funeral. Yet, within days afterward, Frederick William began his work on overhauling the entire Hohenzollern state. First, he cleared up all the unnecessary expenditures, starting with the court. Roughly two-thirds of the courtiers were fired, while the rest received pay cuts. He then sold off all unnecessary belongings, like jewelry, lavish coaches, gold plates, fine wines, and various expensive and exotic animals. The court became barer and rougher, with a notably increased atmosphere of militarism and masculinity. What little social life there was in Frederick William's court revolved around the so-called Tobacco Ministry, a group of roughly ten men, mostly councilors and high-ranking officers, who were sometimes joined by visiting envoys or adventurers. Those guests spent evenings with the king, drinking strong liquors and smoking pipes while discussing topics openly and without concern for the usual court hierarchy. In such an atmosphere, there was no room for female influences like there had been in the Hohenzollern courts for centuries, nor for any kind of formalities that had been so cherished by Frederick I.

Similar cuts and reorientations happened outside the court as well. Artists of various sorts began leaving Berlin, leaving some of their work unfinished. Frederick William also cut the funding of his father's academies. He had little tolerance for expenditures in culture and science, as it showed no immediate practical effect; instead, he thought the money should be spent on the military. Such frugality and martial orientation shined through while he was still a prince. Trying to make the Prussian military more practical, in 1707, young Frederick William proposed more uniformity in the arms and gear the army used. This went from gun caliber and bayonets to cartridge pouches. This would allow for easier supplying and interunit sharing of equipment. He also introduced more rigorous parade drills to his own unit, increasing its maneuverability and fire focus. After his ascension, such practices spread to the rest of the Brandenburg-Prussian Army. However, these advances pale in comparison with the achievements Frederick William made in the realm of enlarging his army.

Initially, the king tried to swell his military by forced recruitment done by his officers. However, the use of fear and violence that usually followed such practices quickly exhibited more harm than improvement. By 1714, Frederick William had decided to bolster his recruitment by using logic and order, combined with one's duty toward the state. First, he proclaimed that all able-bodied men had a duty to serve in the army, then he organized regiments by districts or cantons. Units were filled first with volunteers, then supplemented by enlisted men. However, once in the army, men weren't fully removed from their previous lives. They would pass initial training then move into the reserves, where they stayed until retirement. Soldiers would maintain their efficiency by yearly training, which lasted for about two to three months a year, but they would otherwise be free. Thus, military service wouldn't provide much of an economic burden on the state, as reservists could return to their jobs and occupations. With such a policy, Frederick William doubled the size of the Brandenburg-Prussian Army, swelling it to about eighty thousand strong.

Such numbers, combined with a large pool of reservists, meant that his military was the fourth largest in size in Europe. This was rather remarkable considering that Brandenburg-Prussia was tenth in territory and fourteenth in population. With this, his army became self-sufficient in terms of recruitment, while most others still relied upon mercenaries and foreign conscripts. That fact didn't go unnoticed, prompting Frederick William to ban his nobles from entering into foreign service without his specific approval. Prussians were not going to be European mercenaries anymore. Furthermore, he created an institution of a noble cadet school, requiring, more or less, each aristocratic family to give at least one of their members as officers for the army. However, despite occasional objections, most noble families accepted this rather than opposed it. Not only did such a practice give an opportunity for additional income, which was especially important to impoverished aristocrats, it also provided an opportunity to be close to the throne. Thus, this action simultaneously pacified the nobility and directed them to work for the state instead of against it.

Finally, both the aristocratic officer corps and the cantonal system created a heightened sense of honor and duty among the troops. For the nobles, it provided them with an honorable calling, comparable with the aristocratic ideals of the Middle Ages. For the commoners, it created a sense of comradery, as they served with people they knew from their villages and towns. Furthermore, all reservists were required to wear their uniforms in churches and at other important social gatherings, increasing their sense of pride and unity whilst constantly parading symbols of the state. Thus, such prominent militantism increased the nation's sense of loyalty and patriotism. In the end, Frederick William's military reforms were based on the ideas of universal conscription—an ideal that everyone should serve the state. However, that ideal was never fully achieved, as only about one-seventh of eligible men were ever enlisted. Despite that, it set a strong foundation for later military expansion and further reforms for which the Prussian state became famous.

Surprisingly, regardless of the impressive military reforms, Brandenburg-Prussia was only involved in war once during Frederick William's reign. In 1715, he entered the Great Northern War as a Russian ally, attacking Sweden. While the peace with the Swedes was signed in 1720, the actual campaign was more or less done by 1716. During that short period of time, the Hohenzollern king gained the southern part of Swedish Pomerania, most notably the port city of Stettin (modern-day Szczecin). The war itself continued roughly another year before Russia and Sweden signed a peace treaty. With that, Sweden was ousted from Germany and the Baltic coast, which helped to add Prussia's importance as a local ally.

The only other territorial change during Frederick William's reign was the sale of Brandenburg-Prussian colonies in West Africa to the Dutch. For him, colonial adventures were nothing but the fanciful thinking of his predecessors. Thus, despite being nicknamed the "Soldier King" for his reforms, Frederick William I was rather non-belligerent. Such an attitude could be explained by his frugality, as waging war was costly and would most certainly put a dent into his painstakingly built army.

While thriftiness prevented Frederick William from attaining military glory, it motivated him to pursue probably his most impactful legacy: administrative and fiscal reforms. His grandfather, Frederick William, the Great Elector, began transforming the state bureaucracy, yet this momentum was lost during King Frederick I's reign, as he had little interest in such matters. However, King Frederick William I immediately began working on administrative reforms. In a matter of weeks upon his ascension to the throne, he created the General Directory of War and Finance (*Generalfinanzdirektorium*). This was done by merging the Chief Domains Directory, which managed the crown lands, and the Central Revenue Office to form a body that would oversee income from the royal domains. The financial administration was supplemented with the General Commissariat (*Generalkommissariat*), which was tasked with gathering taxes from towns outside of the crown's territories. However, since their jurisdictions and responsibilities often overlapped, the two offices often confronted each other. To solve this problem, in 1723, Frederick William simply merged the two into a "super-ministry" nicknamed the General Directory (*Generaldirektorium*). It was a shortened form of the General Directory of War and Finance.

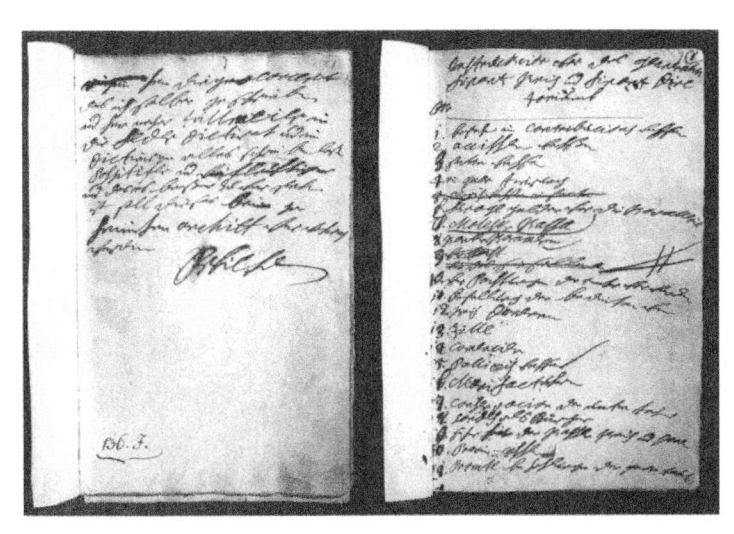

Autographed instruction of Frederick William I of Prussia for the Generaldirektorium. Source: https://commons.wikimedia.org

Despite the unwieldy name, the office was quite thought-out. On top of the bureaucratic chain stood the ministerial college, while below them were several departments filled with numerous councilors. The most important decisions were made in a joint council with all the ministers and related department representatives. A single chair was always left vacant for the king, but he rarely attended those meetings. Nevertheless, collegial decision-making, in theory, minimized the possibility of one misusing their position while also balancing out various local and personal political interests and needs. Despite sounding like a relatively modern bureaucratic apparatus, the General Directory still lacked some improvements. For example, department jurisdictions weren't streamlined. Thus, one department oversaw the territory of Kumark and Magdeburg while also being in charge of provisioning and quartering the troops. Furthermore, with these blurred lines between departments, there were plenty of internal clashes within the directory. Nevertheless, it marked the modernization of the state apparatus.

Such a transformation was important both for increased government revenue and efficiency, as well as for battling the aristocracy's influence. Frederick William purposefully looked at competent commoners to fill various roles in the General Directory, from local positions and offices all the way up to the higher ranks. Thus, he prevented the government from having a sense of solidarity with the nobles. Of course, there were always capable aristocrats willing to assist him in those ventures, whether it was for personal designs or the need for a salary. However, the king in Prussia didn't merely stop there. He found other ways to curb the nobility's power. One was reforming the land taxes. Until his reign, there was a flat rate that was paid per *Hufe* of land owned. A *Hufe* was a measure of land, similar to the medieval English hide, roughly thirty modern acres. Such taxation ignored the yield variations of farmable lands, and the tax-collecting was also still mostly in the hands of the nobles, who often turned a blind eye to each other.

To rectify this, Frederick William ordered a comprehensive landholding survey. This important task exposed some 35,000 previously untaxed *Hufen*, roughly 2,300 square miles (6,000 square kilometers). Then, a local administration officer went on to create a wide classification list of all the holdings according to their soil quality, allowing for fairer taxation. Finally, the taxation was slowly transferred from the hands of the nobles to the central government. Such reforms not only increased the state's income but also helped the growth of agriculture, as pressure was relieved from the poorest smallholders to the major landowners, who were usually aristocrats. The changes also represented the change in ruling and economic theory. Like many other German economists of the time, Frederick William felt that overtaxation reduced productivity. At the same time, the king felt that one of his duties as a sovereign was to protect his subjects, so he began focusing more on the peasants.

Finally, Frederick William dealt another major blow to the leftovers of the feudal era by once again targeting the nobility's power. While the land was being surveyed, he began the process known as the "allodification of the fiefs." In essence, it was the process of de-feudalization, as the royal bureaucracy planned to clear any residual feudal ties between the crown and the landowners. By legally owning the lands, all historical claims would be lifted, allowing for greater freedoms and incentives for agricultural improvements. However, in return, the owners had to pay taxes. This, once again, targeted mostly the aristocracy, who held various contracts and exemptions given for various reasons in previous centuries. Frederick William made that kind of disregard toward tradition clear from the moment he ascended the throne, as he refused to sign the usual concessions to the provincial aristocracy. In his eyes, such leeway given to the nobles eroded the absoluteness of the monarchical reign, which was, in the end, his ultimate goal.

Apart from administrative and martial reforms, Frederick William also worked on bolstering the economy. Apart from the already mentioned agricultural incentives through taxes and allodial reforms, he followed the basic principles of mercantilism, though in a somewhat different form than the original French economic policy. The king sought to protect local farmers by imposing high import taxes on wheat and cracking down on smuggling. Additionally, he banned the export of wool in an attempt to bolster the local textile industry, which was, at the time, the British Industrial Revolution's main motor. In essence, he wanted to lower the imports and make the Prussian economy more reliable and self-reliant. The main difference from more conventional mercantilists was that Frederick William was focused more on agriculture than manufacturing, and he also ignored the advantages of trade. The complete disregard of foreign trade can be seen in his handling of the African colonies. In internal affairs, he was somewhat interested. During Frederick William's rule, the construction of a system of canals between the Oder and Elbe Rivers was sped up, and he also worked on decreasing internal trade tolls. However, the market unification of all the Brandenburg-Prussian territories was never achieved.

Another important economic and social policy used by Frederick William was population resettlement and, even more important, welcoming religious refugees. Like any reasonable ruler, he realized empty lands and workshops meant a loss of revenue for the state. Thus, he sought to repopulate the demographically devastated eastern Prussia. That practice had begun while his father was still alive, but the new king made it a much more important issue. Thus, the crown provided help for internal migration. Later on, in 1732, he allowed Protestant refugees from Salzburg, roughly twenty thousand of them, to settle. In roughly the same period, Prussia accepted some Bohemian refugees, settling them near Berlin. Like in previous times, these people brought their expertise and skills, creating a small economic boost to the lands they settled. Such policies were not new for Brandenburg-Prussia, but they show the Hohenzollerns' religious tolerance while also filling the losses caused by the plague.

Ordinance on the introduction of compulsory schooling in Prussia in 1717.
Source: https://commons.wikimedia.org

Overall, when judging Frederick William I's reign, one can see it was clearly guided by logic, frugality, and absolutism. He wanted to control every aspect of life in his lands, and he worked diligently, demanding the same from his subordinates. Yet, he never forgot the needs of his subjects, great or small. Thus, he expanded granaries, allowing for more stable prices of grain and ensuring there was no more famine. However, his education policy probably shined the most light on his statesmanship. As it was said, he wasn't very concerned with higher education and culture. To him, it was a waste of money. At the same time, he deemed basic education a necessity for a more productive and ordered society. Thus, in 1717, he proclaimed compulsory basic education, being among the first such acts in history. He wanted his subjects to be able to read, write, and do basic math, and he wasn't afraid to order their children to attend school. Though today that seems like a normal part of life, at the time, it was a serious intrusion of family privacy and parenthood. This was absolute control in the name of efficiency.

A 19th-century representation of the Long Lads Battalion in an infantry charge. Source: https://commons.wikimedia.org

Nevertheless, even a king like Frederick William I allowed had illogical and wasteful ideas. For Frederick William, it was the royal guard nicknamed the Long Lads (*Lange Kerle*), which was composed of men at least 6 feet, 2 inches (1.88 meters) tall. Even today, such height is above average, but at the time, such height was even rarer. In comparison, the king himself was 5 foot, 3 inches (1.60 m), which was more comparable with the average height. Thus, gathering some three thousand men of such stature required investment and a "manhunt" across Europe, from England to Ukraine. Not only was it expensive to bring them to Prussia, but the king also gave them higher salaries and some other benefits. Worst of all, most of them were unfit for actual military duty due to their gigantism. Thus, they were merely a decoration, fit for parades and impressing foreign dignitaries. Despite that, there were many accounts of Frederick William finding solace and joy in watching them march up and down his courtyard.

In the end, King Frederick William I was later seen as a spiritual father of the Prussian state, establishing its administrative and military backbone and allowing for its later expansion. However, by the late 1730s, the king grew ill. He was plagued by gout, which had been brought on by his drinking and genetic disposition, rendering him almost bound to a wheelchair. Frederick William passed away in May of 1740 at the age of fifty-one, most likely from heart failure. He was buried as he lived, in a simple metal sarcophagus without any decorations on it. Nevertheless, the success and reforms of his reign continued to resonate with greatness, inspiring his successors to follow in his footsteps.

Chapter 4 – Changing Society

By the mid-18th century, Brandenburg-Prussia was a rather transformed nation. Over roughly a century and three generations of Hohenzollern rulers, it had moved away from its medieval roots into modernity. It was a rather intentional and purposefully constructed change. However, this trend occurred across Europe, making Prussia just one of the states going through reforms, albeit with their own local uniqueness.

One of the major differences between Brandenburg-Prussia and most of the other European states was its fluid religious policy. Compared to other nations, it seemed quite relaxed, though not without its questionable moments. Complications began in 1613 when John Sigismund accepted Calvinism, making it the official religion of the Hohenzollern dynasty. At the time, the majority in Brandenburg were Lutheran, although there were some remnants of Catholics as well. Since religion played an important role in the people's lives, the two schools of Protestantism quickly clashed over their interpretations of Christianity. Some of the notable differences lay in the ideas of predestination and God's sovereignty. For Lutherans, anyone could attain salvation, and humans had some control over their lives. On the other hand, Calvinists believed that people were preselected for salvation and that God had absolute dominion over one's life.

However, although these religious ideas were important to them, this struggle also had a political motivation. Calvinism quickly became the faith of the central government, while the provincial nobility clung to Lutheranism, connecting the religious dispute with the struggle for power and sovereignty.

This prompted Frederick William, the Great Elector, to issue an edict in 1664, proclaiming religious tolerance and forcing towns to accept citizens regardless of their faith. It was an attempt to reconcile the two major congregations. Though forcibly enacted, the edict eased some tensions. However, it wasn't a universal tolerance. Most notably, the Jewish population continued to suffer great religious pressure, which began in the late 16th century. They were expelled from Brandenburg at the time, but with later territorial acquisitions, some smaller communities in Cleve once again fell under the Hohenzollern rule. Nevertheless, the Great Elector chose not to persecute them, but they weren't allowed to move to the electorate. However, in 1671, he allowed a small group of wealthy Jews fleeing from the Habsburgs to settle there. Catholics also had some limits on their faith, though no great purges were ever made. Yet, despite that, Brandenburg-Prussia was still seen as a relatively tolerant state in the late 17th and early 18th centuries. The only actual pressure made by the Hohenzollern rulers was by settling Calvinist emigrants, which, besides economic benefits, bolstered their numbers in a still predominantly Lutheran state.

Yet, despite the ruling dynasty's effort to reconcile Calvinists and Lutherans, discontent brewed beneath the surface. Then, in the late 17th century, a new branch of Lutheranism appeared in Brandenburg-Prussia. It became known as Pietism, and though it still rested on similar principles as the orthodox Lutherans, they argued that faith was individual, that it comes from within, and that, ultimately, there was no need for theological debate. In practice, this made them much more tolerable to other denominations than the "proper" Lutherans. Sensing an opportunity, Frederick III (later King Frederick I), who was just an elector at the time, embraced them and even helped the

Pietists to establish a university in Halle in 1691. This helped Pietism to establish itself, but it also gave the Hohenzollerns new Lutheran allies. It's worth noting that Halle was the largest city in Magdeburg, a region that was a bastion for orthodox Lutherans and opponents of Calvinism. Within a couple of years, Pietist ideas began to spread, and it did, in fact, slightly dull the Lutherans' edge.

Apart from religious policy, Pietism brought other benefits to the state. From their early days in Halle, they were rather active in various social services, providing shelter and food for the poor, creating herbal medicines, and, most importantly, offering free education for the lowest members of society. The latter created foundations for the education system that would spread across Prussia. It was all part of their concern for their fellow Christians and an attempt to create a better society. Thus, the collaboration between the crown and the Pietists continued in the early 18th century. It picked up even more speed with Frederick William I's ascension to the throne. As a child, he had close contact with them and became rather sympathetic to some of their idealized virtues, such as frugality, self-discipline, modesty, and austerity. Those resonated with his visions for a proper society. During his reign, Pietism came under special focus. The king promoted it almost anywhere he could, from bureaucratic apparatus, across the education system, and even in his precious army. They proved to be a significant part of his personal goal to change Brandenburg-Prussia during his rule.

However, the Pietists never managed to overtake other congregations. Their expansion stopped after Frederick William died in 1740, as they had lost their royal support. Even worse, by then, they had lost most of their prominent leaders. Pietism, as a religious movement, lost its momentum. Nevertheless, its cultural importance cannot be underestimated. Though it had a religious core, Pietism put ethics above dogma. It valued punctuality, order, diligence, and modesty, which would all become Prussian core values. Thanks to their ties with education, both in its spreading and reform, these beliefs were spread across the nation. This was, of course, done in no small degree thanks to Frederick William's design. In the end, it was thanks to Pietism that Brandenburg-Prussia laid the ground for the future hallmarks of Prussian and German society while simultaneously paving the path for progressive ideas that would come with the Enlightenment in the latter half of the 18th century.

These ideas and education in general were instrumental in transforming Prussian urban society. The story of this change begins with the authoritarian reforms of the 17th century. However, it is important to realize that the lands ruled by the Hohenzollerns weren't as urban as in some other European regions. For example, around 1700, Brandenburg-Prussia had only two cities with a population of about ten thousand or more: Berlin and Königsberg (modern-day Kaliningrad). Nevertheless, there were dozens of small towns across the Hohenzollern state with their own specific societal milieu. These were run by local master artisans and merchants and were interconnected to form an urban patrician familial network. Their unique identity was garnished by the privileges and degree of autonomy they inherited from medieval times, as cities in Europe generally laid on the edge of the sovereign's control. Thus, the cities were traditionally centers of civic virtues and political self-rule that contrasted to the monarchical system. As the Hohenzollerns strived toward an absolutist reign, towns were their opposition just as much as the nobles.

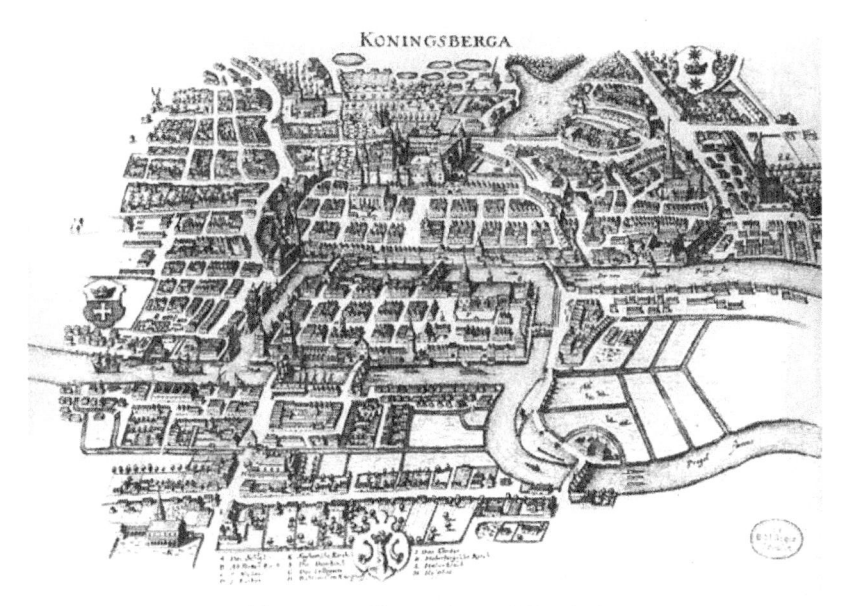

A 17th-century illustration of Königsberg.
Source: https://commons.wikimedia.org

However, since the Prussian towns were smaller and weaker, in both political and monetary terms, they proved to be an easier target for the reforms. Their independence was first targeted by the Great Elector, who decided to impose an excise tax on goods and services in the 1660s. As these were collected at the point of sale or service, it took away the need for fiscal negotiation with the urban elites. The political disenfranchisement caused by this was only furthered in 1667 when the crown began appointing royal tax commissioners in cities. As in other aspects, the centralization of the state slowed during Frederick III/I's reign, but with Frederick William I's ascension to the throne, it picked up the pace. In 1714, he ordered that the urban budgeting authority be transferred to royal officials, further curtailing the powers of town magistrates. Additionally, the king also began to abolish previously set privileges and constitutions of towns across Brandenburg-Prussia, ending their communal independence. His son and heir, King Frederick II, continued his work, expanding the royal control of cities by taking over policing and property control from urban magistrates.

Many historians tend to focus on these aspects in claims that the Hohenzollerns actively tried to destroy the independent civic spirit of towns. While this is partially true, as obedience and loyalty were especially important to Frederick William, it is just part of the whole picture. The transformation was, in essence, motivated by financial gain. To a degree, curbing the political power seemed more secondary, at least in the initial wave of reforms. Furthermore, the urban loss of influence was probably caused more by the economic decline of the towns. This was indeed largely caused by the new taxation policy but not intentionally. The excise tax was supposed to cover both the urban centers and countryside to increase the centralization of the state while also rebalancing the fiscal load since cities paid much higher taxes.

However, since the Great Elector was rather limited by the local aristocracy's power, he was unable to enact taxes in the rural areas. This additionally showcases how less influential the towns were compared to the landed nobility. The difference in taxation created a disparity between the countryside and urban centers. The town's merchants and manufacturers could hardly compete with rural producers who sold their goods duty-free. Limited evidence based on the case of Berlin at the time adds to this claim. The initial response to the excise taxes was the stimulation of the urban economy. Had the tolls been universal, it is possible that the towns would have grown in terms of both wealth and influence, as was the case in most other European nations.

Similar "accusations" of stifling urban voices have been linked with the increased militarization of Brandenburg-Prussia. This comes from the fact that there were many towns that served as garrison centers. On its own, that isn't necessarily intrusive. Yet, the soldiers weren't subject to common law. Thus, military courts also began infringing on the local judiciary systems. Furthermore, local commanders would sometimes become somewhat overbearing, requisitioning supplies and behaving in a paternalistic manner. Finally, some historians even claim that the general militarization of Prussian society led to army-dominated towns where the civic society became passive and lethargic. Such assertions seem to be out of place for several reasons. For one, as mentioned before, soldiers more often than not had enough free time to have additional jobs during their service. If one brought his family along with him, that created additional and much-needed cheap labor to the cities, actually boosting the local economy to a degree. Furthermore, the recruitment laws gave more than decent leeway to the urban population. It exempted many urban young men from service, provided that they were working in some privileged artisan trade or as merchants. Even future academics could escape conscription, sparing the towns from losing their population and workforce.

In cases of both bureaucratic and militaristic "undermining" of urban centers, it seems the truth was somewhat different. Royal officials often became closer to the local population and their interests; in fact, they became part of the town elites. Moreover, it wasn't uncommon for them to become intertwined in town oligarchies and nepotism, proving that the cities weren't fully "subjugated." As for the military, the presence of an army was more symbiotic, never controlling. The fact that city magistrates argued with military commanders over authority issues proves that the urban centers retained their independent civic spirit. In reality, the Hohenzollerns intruded mostly upon traditional privileges and customs, which were leftovers from the medieval era when artisan guilds ruled the cities. It was these disappearing higher classes that were complaining about the crown's treatment. The old system and elites were in the midst of transforming into a new arrangement, one that had a much more entrepreneurial spirit and was content with informal leadership in urban affairs.

*Prussian crown and insignia, symbols of the traditional monarchical power.
Source: htttps://commons.wikimedia.org*

  Because of that, these leading city elites were quick to give their support to the government's educational edicts and reforms. Most of the towns exhibited a demand for better and broader education, while their magistrates and wealthy folk promptly funded new schools and other educational institutions. They realized that education improved the economic situation and that, through societal reforms, it was becoming a basis of class distinction. As the mid-18th century arrived, the urban elites were no longer artisans and craftsmen but instead lawyers, judges, doctors, pastors, and even teachers. All the while, the rural areas continued their resistance to educational reforms, often led by local aristocrats. This was evident by the continuous necessity to pass schooling edicts, both by Frederick William and his heir. This is an example of how limited the Hohenzollern rule actually was. Almost ironically, the heightened focus on education in urban society led to a rise of anti-authoritarian thought, creating the foundation for future civic ideals that accompanied the Enlightenment. Thus, while the crown infringed on some urban freedoms, it was simultaneously paving the way for its most fierce opponents in the upcoming decades.

  The provincial nobility went through a somewhat contrasting transformation. The so-called Junkers, coming from the medieval Germanic term *jung Herr* ("young lord"), were established when nobles and knights settled on the lands taken from the Slavs. As was the custom at the time, they received land and tax exemptions in return for their military service. Because the crown depended so much on them, they had leverage against their rulers, making them the most influential class in the state. The Junkers' importance was only increased by the fact that across Brandenburg-Prussia, they controlled anywhere between 60 to 40 percent of the lands, depending on the region. This was comparable with England, but it was way above the average of France and Russia, whose percentages were 20 or below. It's worth noting that not all of the aristocratic families had large estates; in fact, most of them were rather small compared to their European peers. Nevertheless, using their influence, they often opposed any reforms that curtailed their power. Luckily for the Hohenzollerns, the Junkers of the 17th century were still fragmented and interested only in local affairs, leaving enough space for the crown to maneuver around.

The change in the nature of the Junkers' families came with the militarization of King Frederick William I. Since the nobles were forced to serve in the army and, more importantly, train in the officer corps, the provincial differences began to dissipate. The families from different regions began to intermarry and create connections, making the Junkers a statewide unified class. Theoretically, this should have made them more powerful; however, military service and the possibility of higher salaries through promotions kept many of the less rich nobles loyal. Furthermore, through the cadet school, they were exposed to loyalty-inducing education. From then on, the officer rank became somewhat synonymous with the Junkers. This was only exacerbated during Frederick II's reign, who opposed the promotion of commoners as much as possible. However, the nobility's power was curtailed in the mid-18th century, as an economic crisis and war endangered them. Many of them lost their lives on the battlefield, while others went into debt. Seeking to preserve them, Frederick II created state-backed credit unions. This made many of the Junker families dependent on the state, reversing the balance of power from the 17th century. Thus, from then on, the Junkers became loyal and obedient servants of the Hohenzollern dynasty.

Since the Junkers were an overtly militant class, their representation was usually rather masculine. Their familial ideal was an extended household led by a paterfamilias who would exert his status as the head of the family for the good of the household. With that, it seems there was little space for women to fulfill any significant role besides knitting, gardening, or minding the kitchens. However, there were a number of written sources depicting aristocratic women inheriting estates and taking full control over them. They weren't passive owners nor the legal holder of transferable rights of ownership that would be carried on to their closest male kin. Contrary to expectations, these ladies exercised total control over the estate, developing and investing in it, as well as gathering income; they even served as local judiciaries. However, historical evidence leaves us uncertain about the commonality of these examples. Yet, since the sources never depict women landlords as bizarre or an anomaly, it hints that it was at least socially accepted even if it was not particularly common.

A 1763 portrait of Frederick II. Source: https://commons.wikimedia.org

Interestingly, that kind of status somewhat extended to the commoners as well. Women could be co-owners of estates, especially if it was part of their dowry, while the entire household was usually co-managed in a way that saw wives controlling and managing the family budget. Furthermore, it wasn't uncommon for some better-off commoners to acquire enterprises for their wives, most notably taverns, giving them semi-independency and increasing their social status. However, this doesn't mean there was anything really near equality as we know it today, but rather that, in some ways, Prussian society was a bit more liberal than others at the time. There were still quite stark differences; for example, in the case of adultery and illegitimate children, it was usually seen as the women's fault. Furthermore, city guilds were usually closed to females, making it almost impossible for them to advance in urban artisanal industries.

In the countryside, the division between male and female labor was less pronounced, and both sexes worked on the fields as needed. However, as the 18th century was coming to an end, it seems that Prussian society was slowly transforming to a much more conservative one, stifling these hints of equality.

Another unique development in Prussian society was the position of peasants. In the mid-15th century, the Junkers first restructured their estates so that the best land was under their direct control while simultaneously increasing their level of control over their dependents. Most notably, they imposed forced labor and forbade them from leaving the lands. Thus, while the rest of Europe was abandoning feudalism, in Brandenburg-Prussia, there was something close to a feudal revival, albeit with one major distinction. Peasants weren't true serfs since they didn't legally belong to their masters. Such a level of dominion over their subjects often bordered and crossed into tyranny, leaving peasants in poverty and apathy. However, by the 17th century, these conditions began to change, mostly thanks to the state's intervention. Both the Great Elector and his grandson sought to protect the commoners from unjust treatment by their masters. This was done by intertwining the local laws with statewide regulations. Then, Frederick II took it a step beyond by requiring the territorial courts to employ university-educated judges.

It is also vital to note that even without state protection, not all peasants were repressed and abused. There were many cases where, with proper estate management, many Junker families managed to create incentives for work, such as paid labor, which instilled some sense of entrepreneurship among the peasants. On the other side of the spectrum were estates where peasants grouped together to rebel against their lieges. In several instances, the commoners were strong enough to refuse to pay taxes or do proscribed labor. However, these weren't uprisings against the Junkers' rule but rather demonstrations due to unfair treatment, usually the unlawful increase of duties. What seems to be common for all these rebellions was the commoners' utmost trust that the judicial system would ultimately protect them against the oppression of their masters. Another way of peaceful resistance was neglecting the land, which created an impetus for the landowners to employ paid labor and fairer treatment.

Furthermore, by the mid-18th century, there was a considerable number of free peasants. Most of these were settlers and migrants, as well as their descendants. They were most prominent in eastern Prussia because of the plague in the early 18th century. By the end of the century, more than 20 percent of the peasants there were non-subjugated farmers. Overall, it seems that the Hohenzollerns "used" the commoners to further curtail the power of the Junkers, dismantling remnants of feudalism along the way. Immigrants played an additional role in Brandenburg-Prussia. The Hohenzollerns used them to boost manufacturing and industry. Some of them were industrious and versed in such matters, creating a base for further development. However, the crown did more than just invite manufacturers and experts to their lands. Most notably, the state tried to prevent the export of raw materials, giving local producers resources to work with. Besides that, the government and the ruler sought to give subsidies and aid for starting or developing industries in the towns.

First among them was the textile-related industries, namely wool and silk. Then came the leather industry, followed by various factories related to metal products like scissors, knives, and even munition. All this was further boosted with the formation of the iron ore industry after Frederick II gained more territories. All of these industries were heavily protected by import tariffs but also suffered from governmental guidance. According to some historians and even contemporaries, as much as state investments had helped set up the industries, they began to stifle Prussia's progress by the late 18th century. However, despite their claims and even under such conditions, the Prussian industry wasn't really stagnating, nor was it under the all-encompassing control of the state. Most of the factories were privately held, even those connected with military needs, while production continuously increased despite complaints of governmental interloping. Even more important, state funding allowed for the previously economically devastated Brandenburg-Prussia to create a foundation for its later industrial rebirth, allowing Prussia to catch up with British industrial might that was brought about in the 18th-century Industrial Revolution. Furthermore, it led to the formation of a new economic elite, which included industrials, bankers, subcontractors, and distributors.

Overall, when following the trends in the Brandenburg-Prussian society and state, it seems that the late 17th and early 18th centuries was a period of transforming into a modern nation. Some of the changes were intentional, some unintended, but most were connected with the Hohenzollerns' underlying desire to increase either their economic and military power. Despite that, it should be mentioned that, in the larger picture, similar changes were happening across all of western Europe.

Chapter 5 – Pride and Glory

The transformation of the Prussian state and society in the late 17th and early 18th centuries hinted at a new reservoir of power behind the Hohenzollern dynasty. Through various reforms and improvements, a seed of greatness was sown. The first of its blossoms were to bloom with Frederick William's son, King Frederick II, better known as Frederick the Great.

As with his predecessors, the story of Frederick's reign begins with familial traumas during his formative years. While he was still a child, he exhibited a fondness for reading, arts, and philosophy, and he was much less concerned with military issues and certainly less blunt than his father. This irritated Frederick William, who thought that his son and heir should be as close as possible to his mirror image. Hence, the two began constantly clashing. The father imposed a grueling routine upon his son, forcing him to deal with stately affairs before he even became a teenager. When the treatment showed little effect, Frederick William became increasingly frustrated, and he was prone to engage in public ridicule and violence at the expense of his heir. In return, Frederick became colder and more distant; although he was outwardly supportive of his father, privately, he became more inclined toward his own interests. Then, in the late 1720s, young Frederick became a focal point of political machinations in the court. His mother sought to arrange a marriage with Princess Amelia of Britain, but several ministers opposed it. They were most likely bribed by the Habsburgs to prevent such an alliance.

Frederick II (on the window) watching the execution of his friend Katte. Source: https://commons.wikimedia.org

Frederick William I quickly opposed the marriage, fearing the break with Vienna, while Frederick decided to support his mother's plot. In the end, though, the king's word was final, and the queen had to back down. For his son, this was a tipping point, not because he really cared for Princess Amelia but because of his resentment for his father's actions and treatment of him. This prompted Frederick to attempt to flee the country with the help of a friend and Prussian officer named Hans Hermann von Katte. However, they were caught and imprisoned in the Küstrin fortress. Frederick was sentenced to imprisonment on charges of treason. He would remain at Küstrin, condemned to go through rigorous training in governance and administration. Yet, the true punishment was the execution of his friend and co-conspirator, which he was forced to watch. It showed the extent of his father's cold-heartedness. Despite that, the two worked on reconciling in the following years. In 1732, Frederick was released and reinstituted on the condition he would marry a bride of his father's choosing.

Frederick accepted, but he warned that he would "reject" his wife. Over the next several years, his relationship with Frederick William improved, most notably because his father eased up on him. Frederick was given a castle near Berlin, where he spent most of his time until his ascension to the throne. There, he continued to enjoy and practice the arts, philosophy, and writing, living a life that almost resembled freedom. He didn't only enjoy the works of others but also dabbled in philosophic works, music, and poetry himself. He also worked on political tracts, most notably his essay, the *Anti-Machiavel*, as well as historical manuscripts, such as the *History of House of Brandenburg*. This solidified his erudite personality. It also gave him the possibility to comprehend his role and position in the development of Prussia and the Hohenzollern dynasty. It also allowed him to develop less desirable personality traits for an 18th-century ruler. Frederick became an atheist, claiming that Christianity was merely metaphysical fiction filled with contradictions and absurdities. He was also rumored to be homosexual or at least more inclined to men than women. Such gossip began even during his lifetime, and it is still a highly debated topic even today.

Partially, this was because he remained cold toward his wife, Elisabeth. After 1740, Frederick and Elisabeth had basically separated, though they never divorced. She was sidelined in a single castle, retaining all her official titles and prerogatives, but she was never accepted as part of her husband's social circle. Making matters worse, they never produced an heir, and it seems that their relationship never got to a sexual level. Another conspicuous act was that even after becoming the king, Frederick abstained from having mistresses. That would be a viable "way out" if the marriage was too important to be dissolved. Adding to the speculations was Frederick's inclination toward male company. On its own, this wouldn't be too damning. Even Frederick William had his Tobacco Ministry. However, Frederick's inner circle was less macho-orientated, filled with gentler types like poets and philosophers. Most notoriously, all of them, including the king, dabbled in erotic poetry and essays, some of which hinted at dubious feelings of attraction. Eyebrow-raising relations with the famous philosopher Voltaire only added to the slander. The two of them had rather feisty relations, filled with mutual appreciation and constant bickering. After a falling out, Voltaire even claimed that Frederick enjoyed the company of his lackeys and cadets, though he never went "all the way."

These claims of homosexuality were vigorously combated by German writers and memoirists, who talked about Frederick's mistresses in his youth, hinting that he was heterosexual at the time. In the end, the reality of Frederick's sexuality remains a mystery. It is entirely possible he was either bisexual or asexual, with the latter possibly being the result of his father's ill-treatment. In that case, his sexuality toward both genders would be only artistic and intellectual.

However, the matter of Frederick's sexuality remains less important, as it pales in comparison to his grand achievements. The first glimpses of Frederick's greatness came in 1740, within a few months of him ascending to the throne. In contrast to the peaceful reign of his father, the "Soldier King," twenty-eight-year-old Frederick II began his rule with a declaration of war against the Habsburgs.

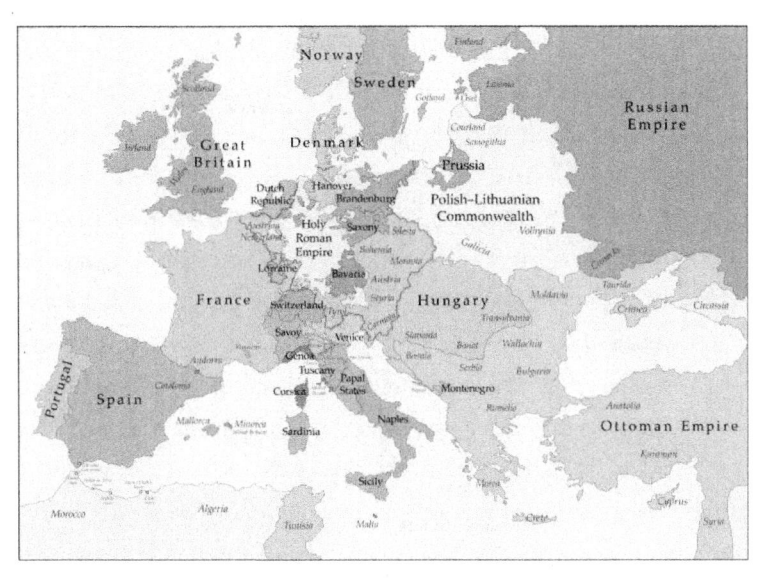

A map of Europe in 1740. Source: https://commons.wikimedia.org

Despite being mocked for his lack of military prowess, King Frederick II realized that the time was ripe to attack Austria. Firstly, the Habsburgs' treasury was running dry after having lost a couple of their previous wars. When Frederick was still the crown prince, he took part in one of them as a leader of a Prussian contingent. It allowed him to witness firsthand how inferior the Austrian army was compared to his father's troops. Moreover, in late 1740, Emperor Charles VI died, leaving only daughters. His principal heir was Maria Theresa, whose right to inherit as a female was questionable, to say the least, as Habsburgs law dictated male primogeniture. Her father tried to secure Maria's inheritance with an edict, but that wasn't enough to restrain numerous Austrian opponents. This added to Frederick's opportunity; not only would other German dynasties try to achieve gains, but he knew that France wouldn't mind if the Habsburgs were taken down a notch. Furthermore, Britain and Russia, which were chief Austrian allies, were preoccupied with their own issues.

Thus, acting quickly, in December 1740, Frederick started the so-called First Silesian War, named after Prussia's primary target. He attacked, acting on flimsy Hohenzollern claims on Silesia that dated back to the 16th and early 17th centuries. However, these were just a pretext for a war of pure aggression. The real reason Silesia was his primary target came from the fact that it was the only Habsburg region bordering Brandenburg-Prussia. Adding to that was the fact that it was lightly defended, as the majority of the Habsburg troops were deployed elsewhere. It was only a bonus that it was also the richest and most valuable Habsburg province, yielding high taxes and a rather developed industry. The final motive was the threat of Saxony trying to conquer Silesia. This would, in turn, threaten Brandenburg, as it would connect Saxony and Poland, which were under the personal union of Frederick Augustus from the Wettin dynasty. If the Wettins took Silesia, they would more or less encircle the Hohenzollerns, making their future questionable, to say the least.

The war began auspiciously. The Prussian troops easily swept the Habsburg defenders, taking control of almost all of Silesia by January 1741. In the spring, the Austrians gathered for a counterattack. They had some minor success, but in the Battle of Mollwitz, their momentum was broken by a Prussian victory. At that moment, other European nations felt the Habsburgs' weakness. An alliance between France, Spain, Bavaria, and Saxony was formed, along with Brandenburg-Prussia. The allies confirmed Frederick's claim and conquest, and their entrance started a much larger conflict known as the War of the Austrian Succession. The campaigns continued throughout late 1741 and early 1742, with the Prussian Army playing an active role in it. However, by the summer, Frederick sensed it was enough for him and Prussia. He had achieved his goal and wasn't keen on totally dismembering Austria to replace it with some other new power. Thus, he negotiated a separate peace through the treaties of Breslau and Berlin. Maria Theresa had little choice but to cede Silesia to the Hohenzollerns.

Despite gaining roughly one million new subjects and around 14,000 square miles (35,000 square kilometers), Frederick continued to monitor the situation in the ongoing European conflict. He was wary of a possible renewed threat from Austria, as he was certain it wasn't going to abandon Silesia that easily. By mid-1744, Frederick realized his position might be threatened. The war had turned. France had suffered severe setbacks, while Austria formed alliances with Britain, Russia, and Saxony. Frederick was aware he had to act quickly. After signing some more treaties with France and other Germanic states, Prussia reentered the arena. This renewed conflict became known as the Second Silesian War. Initially, it seemed it was going to be a repeat of the first campaign, as the Prussians managed to quickly invade Habsburgian Bohemia, taking Prague in the process. However, due to France's weakness at the time, the Austrians managed to redeploy their soldiers back to the east. Faced by the joint Austro-Saxon army, as the latter became an active belligerent, by November 1744, Frederick was forced to retreat. This not only harmed his military reputation but also cost him a substantial chunk of his army, as low supplies and illnesses reduced it by half.

A later painting of the Battle of Hohenfriedberg.
Source: https://commons.wikimedia.org

In early 1745, the Austrians refocused on subduing Bavaria before once again targeting Prussia with their Saxon allies. Frederick waited for them with a replenished army in Silesia. The first major encounter happened in June at the Battle of Hohenfriedberg. Both armies were roughly the same size, around sixty thousand, but the Prussians' training and Frederick's command tipped the scale in his favor. The Austro-Saxon army fled, and Frederick went on the pursuit. However, over the next two months, no major battles occurred as he tried to secure another peace that would confirm Prussian control over Silesia. However, Maria Theresa wasn't ready to give up yet, even though she was losing British support due to their own internal issues at the time. Then, in late September, the Austro-Saxon army decided to challenge the pursuers. By then, the Prussian Army had less than twenty-five thousand men, making it seem like perfect prey for the forty thousand Austro-Saxon troops. The latter even tried to make their clash a surprise attack near the village of Soor. Despite all of their disadvantages, the Prussian troops still managed to win the battle. Frederick hoped that this defeat would be enough for the Habsburgs to sue for peace, but their resolve was unscathed.

While the Prussians retreated to Silesia to regroup and resupply, the Austrians and Saxons agreed to take the war to Brandenburg. Their goal was to seize Berlin and end the war altogether. However, Frederick got wind of their plans, and he arranged for a new defensive army in his homeland while silently following the Austro-Saxons with his army. He waited until they arrived at the Brandenburgian border before attacking them in late November. The Battle of Hennersdorf was yet another crushing defeat for the coalition forces. Frederick's other army then marched into Saxony, with both Prussian forces converging on its capital of Dresden. The second Prussian force then found a smaller army of mostly Saxon soldiers on its way. Despite being slightly outnumbered, with thirty-five thousand Austro-Saxons against some thirty-two thousand Prussians, the latter decided to attack. Once again, Prussian leadership and troop quality led to a crushing victory in mid-December 1745 at the Battle of Kesselsdorf. A few days later, the Prussian troops entered Dresden. There was no other option for the Austro-Saxon alliance than to accept Frederick's terms.

Mediated by the British, the Treaty of Dresden was signed on December 25th, 1745, ending the Second Silesian War. The end result was another confirmation of Prussian gains in Silesia, which had been Frederick's primary goal, and the Saxons also had to pay a hefty indemnity. In return, Prussia acknowledged Maria Theresa's husband as the emperor. The grander conflict of the War of the Austrian Succession lasted for almost another three years, ending in late 1748. That peace treaty once again confirmed that Silesia was now Prussian, despite the fact that it wasn't involved in the war, nor was Frederick even one of the signees. By now, Frederick II was gaining his nickname "the Great," as he shocked the other powers with his decisive victories. Just a few years before, it was unimaginable that the third-rate power of Brandenburg-Prussia would be able to beat one of the leading world powers, the Habsburgs. This caused a ripple effect in the rearranging of alliances, as Prussia had emerged as one of the leading Germanic powers, directly challenging Habsburgian dominance within the Holy Roman Empire.

The most notable change was that Maria Theresa decided to go against the Habsburg traditions and tried to align itself with France rather than Britain. This caused the so-called Diplomatic Revolution, as the main axis of alliances was aligned around long-lasting hostilities between the Habsburgs and the French Bourbons. This change was done partially when Austria realized its interests and geopolitical position were vastly different than Britain. However, it was also partially aimed against Prussia. Regaining Silesia became one of the Habsburgs' primary goals, not only for its economic importance but also for the loss of prestige. While the alliances slowly shifted, the French and British began clashing over their colonial possessions in North America. Britain anticipated a full-out war and concluded a treaty with Russia to attack Prussia in order to halt Frederick as a French ally from taking over Hanoverian lands on the continent. This alarmed the king in Prussia, who immediately tried to negotiate a deal with the British. Thus, by early 1756, Brandenburg-Prussia became a British ally and swore to protect King George II's lands in Hanover.

It was a rash action, mostly caused by Frederick's gross fear of a Russian invasion. He miscalculated his move so much that it played straight into the vengeful hands of the Habsburgs. The French saw it as a betrayal of their continuing alliance, while the Russians were angry about the treatment. Both were ready to ally with Austria against Prussia. A storm was brewing on the horizon, and Frederick II was aware of it. In mid-1756, he tried to gain guarantees that the gathering Russian and Austrian armies were aimed against Prussia, but none were given. He now realized that an invasion was imminent, with it most likely coming in early 1757. He decided not to wait. In August 1756, Prussia invaded Saxony, kicking off the Third Silesian War, which was, in turn, part of a much wider conflict known as the Seven Years' War. This gave the Austro-Russian coalition a diplomatic excuse to attack. They were joined by Saxony, whose participation wasn't yet formalized at the time but was expected, as well as Sweden, which dreamed of taking back Pomerania. On the other hand, only Portugal decided to side with Britain and Prussia, while the other less powerful Germanic states formed two opposing blocs, depending on their interests and positions.

When the war started, Prussia found itself fighting for survival. If the Austro-Russian coalition's plans were to come true, the Hohenzollerns would be left only with Brandenburg. Looking at the opposition forces, it seemed like Frederick had little chance to win. Unlike the two previous Silesian wars, this one wasn't a string of Prussian victories. Instead, in the sixteen major battles, only half were won by Frederick. However, each victory was enough to keep Prussia afloat. This played to his hand because, apart from Maria Theresa, the other enemies weren't so upset at Frederick II. Thus, France remained mostly preoccupied with its Atlantic struggle against Britain. Its commitment was further tested when a Prussian force of twenty thousand inflicted a crushing defeat on a French-Austrian force twice that size at the Battle of Rossbach in November of 1757. It was actually the only direct confrontation between French and Prussian troops, but it was enough for the former to decide to become only a financial ally to the coalition beginning in March of 1758. At roughly the same time, Britain sent substantial economic aid to its ally, helping Frederick's war effort.

*A contemporary painting of the Battle of Rossbach.
Source: https://commons.wikimedia.org*

This mismatched battle record of Frederick's armies also proved that he wasn't an undefeatable military genius. Although he had a keen tactical mind, he also had his drawbacks. For example, in the Battle of Kunersdorf in August of 1759, Frederick showed his flawed comprehension of how the battle unfolded. He lost more than a third of his army in a decisive defeat against the Austro-Russian forces. Furthermore, some victories proved too costly to yield any actual gains. This can be seen in the Battle of Torgau in November 1760, when roughly fifty thousand Prussians defeated an Austrian army of the same size, with both sides losing some fifteen thousand men. It was a Pyrrhic victory in a strategic sense since Prussia gained little from it. However, it seemed that Frederick was capable of winning when it was necessary, and he had a stunning ability to recover from defeats and inflict crucial blows on his enemies. This was partially due to his military capabilities, which mostly stemmed from him keeping a cool head amidst a crisis, but also because the Prussian military was usually the better-trained force on the battlefield.

In the end, it seemed that time worked in Frederick's favor, though it may not have seemed like that at the time. As the war dragged on, with all nations suffering from exhaustion, Austria's allies started to flake. First, Russia withdrew from the war in early 1762 after a change on its throne. They were quickly followed by Sweden, who had no strength to fight the Prussians on their own and were too far away from the Habsburgs. By the December of that year, representatives from Saxony, Austria, and Prussia began their own negotiations. These were only hastened when France and Britain signed their own peace, with Saxony, Austria, and Prussia concluding their treaty on February 15th, 1763, at Hubertusburg Castle. Under its provisions, *status quo ante bellum* was reinforced, which had been Frederick's only real goal. In addition, Austria publicly denounced its claim on Silesia, and, in return, Frederick vowed to vote for Maria Theresa's son in the upcoming imperial elections.

The Third Silesian War is usually depicted as a Prussian victory. And, on most accounts, it was, as Frederick managed to hold on to his previous gains and repel a powerful coalition that wanted to dismember his state. However, it was a costly victory. In the simplest terms, it emptied the Prussian treasury. It was even costlier in terms of human lives. All the major battles left armies with thousands killed in action, with many more perishing from hunger, diseases, or succumbing to battle wounds along the way. According to some rough estimates, some 180,000 Prussian soldiers lost their lives in combat. Even worse, throughout the war, most Prussian territories were invaded by enemy forces. The occupation wasn't as traumatizing as during the Thirty Years' War, as the majority of troops were now more disciplined and supplied by their states, yet the local population still suffered. Invading armies extorted money and supplies, and there were also cases of war atrocities, such as pillaging, murder, and rape.

These were mostly done by the irregular "light troops," which were filled with volunteers and were semi-autonomous auxiliary units of the main army.

If the direct violence wasn't enough, occupied lands also suffered from food shortages and, even worse, various epidemics that the armies brought with them. These diseases likely accounted for most of the civilian deaths. It is important to note that the Prussian armies brought the same misery to the enemy lands they occupied. That was just a part of war in the 18th century. It was mostly unavoidable, as armies were a burden even on their own territories. Nevertheless, when the civilian casualties are added up, Brandenburg-Prussia lost some 400,000 people during the war. That is roughly 10 percent of its population, a terrible blow to its demographics and, in turn, the economy. The loss of lives, coupled with the destruction and pillaging of the invaders, left many farms abandoned, and there was also a substantial amount of damaged property and infrastructure. Thus, these should also be accounted for when measuring the success of Prussia's participation in the Third Silesian War.

In the end, besides preserving its borders and losing hundreds of thousands of lives, Prussia also gained something its rulers had coveted for a long time. Its position as a great power was acknowledged by the other European nations, even though it was still not on the same level as, for example, France or Britain. Through the three wars for Silesia, Frederick finally accumulated enough recognition and glory for himself, the Prussian state, and the Hohenzollern dynasty.

Chapter 6 – From Glory to Humiliation

Despite what seemed like a magnificent victory against overwhelming odds, Frederick the Great wasn't ready to relax and enjoy the fruits of his conquests. Being the keen statesmen he was, the Prussian king was aware that Brandenburg-Prussia was devastated, in need of recuperation, and, most of all, not yet safe.

After 1763, Frederick turned toward rebuilding and repopulating his state. Like his predecessors, he lured immigrants to the depopulated regions, promising them lands to live and work on. He also financed the building of a canal system, which drained marshy lands previously unavailable for farming. In turn, the same canals would also ease up market integration and supply shipping. During his reign, the potato and turnip were introduced in Prussia as a new type of crop, ones better suited to combat famine. To this end, Frederick also reorganized the system of state grain magazines and began actively using the grain excise tax to influence the import of basic foods. With the latter, he first suspended the taxation of all grains in 1766, allowing for cheaper imports from Poland. Then, when the situation bettered, he introduced the excise tax on wheat, which was at the time used by better-situated classes. This way, taxation fell on those with enough money to pay them. In the case of the grain magazines, Frederick used them to release stored grains during times of famine, which was particularly important in 1771 and 1772 when there was a Europe-wide shortage.

A portrait of Frederick II from the 1780s.
Source: https://commons.wikimedia.org

This showed that after the war, Frederick had at least the same amount of attention for social issues as for the military because the primary role of the magazine system was to hold supplies for the army. Similarly, the king also showed surprising care for his veterans. He set up an institution to care for invalids, provided monetary subsidies for poverty-stricken soldiers, and made low-wage jobs at the lowest levels of governmental posts available to those who fought for him and the state. It was his way of repaying those who had risked everything for him.

Apart from welfare, Frederick continued to rebuild and enlarge his army. He was aware that the security of all his gains rested upon the strength of the Prussian Army. His military had some 195,000 soldiers in the last years of his reign, making it officially the third-largest army in Europe, despite being the thirteenth state by population. This meant that roughly 3.4 percent of Prussians were serving. This led to the famous depiction of the Prussian monarchy being a military with a state rather than the other way around.

Nevertheless, Frederick never again committed his troops to any serious warfare. The only time they rode to combat was in the War of the Bavarian Succession. This came about when the Habsburgs tried to seize Bavaria after its ruling dynasty had died out. Prussia and Saxony opposed it, and in mid-1778, it escalated into a war. Frederick once again led his troops, invading Habsburg-held Bohemia; however, no major battle occurred as the two armies maneuvered around each other, succumbing mostly to famine and disease. Neither Frederick nor Maria Theresa, who was now a co-ruler with her son Joseph, wanted this to turn into another bloody conflict, so the war was concluded with a peace treaty in May of 1779. The deal was struck with the mediation of Russia and France. Bavaria was left to a side branch of its previous dynasty, while Austria gained a small territorial compensation along its border with Bavaria. In return, the Habsburgs recognized the Prussian claim on the duchies of Ansbach and Bayreuth, though their acquisition was to come some years later.

The War of the Bavarian Succession confirmed that the Holy Roman Empire was influenced by more than one king. It was no longer solely the Habsburgs' playground; they had to share authority with the Hohenzollerns. However, Frederick's crowning achievement in terms of diplomacy and power status had come a few years before. In the late 1760s, Russia was waging a successful war against the Ottomans. That caused concern in Austria, and it seemed that another major war was brewing on the horizon. The Habsburgs were determined to maintain the perceived balance of power. Such a development was unfavorable for Frederick, as he had become a Russian ally in 1764. So, he turned toward diplomacy, an action that showcased that Frederick's political skills were equal to his military capabilities. He refocused both Austria's and Russia's attention on Poland, which was, at the time, still officially the Polish-Lithuanian Commonwealth. For some time, Poland had been on a downward spiral on a political, military, and economic level. It lost its "major power" status, slowly becoming dependent on other nations, most notably Russia. Because of that, it was the perfect prey.

Frederick, with the help of his brother Henry (Heinrich), entered negotiations with Vienna and Saint Petersburg. He proposed that the three states divide Poland, preserving the balance of power, instead of waging another war over the lands that Russia would take from the Turks. The talks lasted for roughly two years, between 1770 to 1772, until the three sides finally agreed on the so-called First Partition of Poland. However, even before they ended, all three sides began occupying their desired territories. Austria gained the most populated share in the partition, occupying the provinces of Galicia and Lodomeria. Russia took a slightly larger territory, which was mostly located in present-day Belarus and Latvia, though it had a lesser population. Prussia gained the least from the partition, at least in raw numbers. Its territorial gains represented 5 percent of the commonwealth, compared with Russia's 12.7 percent and Austria's 11.8 percent. In it were some 600,000 new subjects, compared with 1.3 million for Russia and 2.6 for Austria. However, it was by far the most important gain strategically, as it consisted of so-called Royal Prussia, without Danzig (Gdańsk), along with two additional border districts. These lands became known as West Prussia, finally connecting East Prussia with Brandenburg. Furthermore, this territory held important economic value because of its ports and developed trade connections.

Taking over Royal Prussia and uniting the entirety of Prussian lands under the Hohenzollern rule allowed for a less palpable but no less important act. In 1772, Frederick II changed his title from "King in Prussia" to the more common monarchical term of "King of Prussia." This was done because, by then, neither Poland nor the Habsburgs could object. It goes without saying that Frederick did this without consulting the emperor in Vienna. He also arranged it so that the titles Duke of Prussia and Elector of Brandenburg were attached to the kingly title. This was purely a display of the sovereignty and autonomy of the newly strengthened Prussian state and its position as being an equal to other European powers. It also helped speed up the process of the "Prussianization" of the Hohenzollern state. As the 18th century drew closer to its final years, contemporaries began avoiding using cumbersome "Brandenburg-Prussia" in favor of "Prussian lands" or simply "Prussia," though the latter was officially accepted only in the early years of the 19th century.

Map of Europe in 1786, with all Prussian gains during Frederick's reign.
Source: https://commons.wikimedia.org

Thus, the lands of the Hohenzollerns began shedding their dualistic nature during Frederick II's reign. From his rule and onward, it would be historically correct to call his lands Prussia. However, all that was merely a titular matter. More important was the fact that his rule also worked to unify the people. Like in many other European nations at the time, a sense of patriotism began to arise, a precursor to the nationalism of the 19th century. In Prussia, it was largely centered around the allegiance to the king, particularly Frederick the Great. Without much aid from his personal actions, a cult of personality was born, and it only grew after his death. Nevertheless, through his personality, his subjects began creating a shared identity under the umbrella term "Prussians," through which people of all classes and backgrounds shared a unifying factor. The loyalty to the king then transitioned to loyalty toward the state, as the two were somewhat synonymous at the time. One's love and devotion to the state were only increased through the wars and joint struggles, helping to create the ideals of dying for one's nation. Of course, like with any feelings of that kind, patriotism created resentment and dislike for other nations. In Prussia's case, it was most notably the Russians and French. However, there was a similar separation between "us and them" with other Germanic states, like Austria, Franconia, or Bavaria.

As for other internal policies, Frederick II acted as an enlightened absolutist, somewhat of a combination of his father and his grandfather. He continued to modernize the state's administration, though not at the same pace as during Frederick William's reign. The long periods of war hampered such developments, but after 1763, there were some actions in that direction. Despite the disdain Frederick II held for his father, he eventually went a step beyond, despite claiming that the king was only the first servant of the state. During his long rule, the entire bureaucratic system revolved around him, and he somewhat disregarded ministers and directories. Every major decision came from the king, and he often worked directly with provincial officials, which led to a certain level of decentralization. According to his idea of "allegiance to the state," Frederick always put the well-being of the state before his personal gains, actively working to protect and develop the industry and economy. Yet, Frederick's absolutism only grew in his later years, prompting Voltaire to denounce him as an enlightened philosopher.

Nevertheless, Frederick retained some central ideas of the Enlightenment. Most notable was his willingness to invest in the arts and science, reopening some of the universities his father had closed. He invited philosophers, artists, and other intellectuals to come to Prussia, hoping to elevate it culturally. Furthermore, the king erected numerous public buildings connected with culture, like the Berlin Opera or Royal Library, both of which are still standing in the German capital. Thanks to Frederick's religious skepticism, he also promoted religious tolerance to a much larger degree than in any of the surrounding states. However, he retained some amount of prejudice, especially toward the Jews, but that never led to any persecutions. In fact, he worked hard to integrate them into the emerging Prussian society. Further developing upon the ideas of the Enlightenment, Frederick granted his subjects a substantial amount of freedom of speech, and he also worked on reforming the judicial system to abolish torture and death sentences. This led to the reorganization of the courts and laws, and he created a unified code of law that would serve the state before anything. However, the General Prussian Code of Law was finished in 1794, several years after his death. All of those facts confirm that, despite his absolutism, Frederick the Great remained faithful to some ideals of the Enlightenment until his final days in 1786.

Frederick II was succeeded by his nephew, Frederick William II, the son of his younger brother, Prince Augustus William (August Wilhelm), who died in 1758. The new king was similar to his illustrious uncle. Frederick William was also quite interested in the arts and played the cello, and he showed signs of a capable intellect. However, he had large shoes to fill, and he lacked any proper training in state affairs. Making matters worse for Frederick William II was the fact that Europe was about to enter one of its most turbulent periods, with the French Revolution and the subsequent Napoleonic Wars. In such trying times, Frederick William's average capabilities simply weren't enough. Trying to prove his worth in comparison to Frederick II, the new king tried to relax taxation and burdens on the people, gaining some popularity while losing economic stability. Furthermore, though he continued to expand the Prussian Army, he chose not to oversee it personally, leaving it under the control of the Supreme College of War. This gave an impetus to the degradation of Prussian military might, as the increase in quantity was paired with a drop in the quality of the troops.

A portrait of Frederick William II. Source: https://commons.wikimedia.org

Despite that, it seems that Frederick William tried to maintain the status of Prussia being a major European power. First, in 1787, he intervened in the Netherlands, supporting the ruling party in a civil war. It was a low-key adventure that brought only expenses without any palpable gains. Then, his focus turned southward to the

Habsburgs, who began a new war against the Ottoman Empire in the Balkans. Since the Turks were already entangled in a conflict against the Russians, the Habsburgs were in a very good position to acquire new territories and restore their dominant position in the Germanic world. Of course, Frederick William wasn't keen on seeing this; thus, when a chain of revolts erupted across the Habsburg Monarchy in 1789, the Prussians were quick to encourage them and even entered into some talks of assisting them. At roughly the same time, France was engulfed in the first wave of its revolution. While most European monarchies condemned it, Prussia remained neutral, verging on supporting it. This was done because there was some liberal support for revolutionaries rebelling against "despotism" in Paris but more because it was disrupting the Habsburg-Bourbon alliance. Austria was losing its major ally, making Prussia's position stronger than before.

At that moment, Prussia's foreign policy began to change. First, the Austrian ruler approached Frederick William. The Habsburg emperor was wary of the possibility of a Prussian-backed insurrection in Hungary, so he proposed to find common ground. In mid-1790, after a long negotiation, the two sides agreed that Austria would abandon all the new lands taken from the Ottomans, while the Prussians would stop encouraging rebellions in the Habsburg lands. It marked the start of Austro-Prussian rapprochement, as the two slowly began turning against the French revolutionaries, who were becoming more and more radical. By mid-1791, the Habsburgs and the Hohenzollerns had become allies, announcing their support for the Bourbon king. The allies then continued to iron out details of their actions against the revolutionaries, which was accompanied by the usual political negotiations on gains and territories. However, even before they could arrange a course of action, revolutionary France declared war on Austria in early 1792. By the summer, the joint Austro-Prussian forces were marching toward France.

Like in the previous similar offensives, the Germanic forces had a rough time coordinating and executing their plans on the western periphery of the Holy Roman Empire. Their effectiveness was only lowered by the resentment of local Frenchmen. The joint force managed to take control of the border fortresses of Longwy and Verdun as they slowly moved toward Paris. Then, in late September, the invading Austro-Prussian force encountered its first real opposition from the revolutionaries at Valmy. Two armies of roughly equal size, around thirty-five thousand men each, faced off in what technically ended in a tactical draw. The two sides exchanged artillery fire before the Germanic forces withdrew. The reason why is unclear, but it seems that the Prussians weren't keen on fighting against well-positioned French defenders. It is possible that they were saving their troops for the new troubles brewing east in Poland. Regardless, the revolutionaries felt the wind in their sails when the joint force retreated. After the Battle of Valmy, Prussia's participation in the war against France was minimal, although some of their troops continued to participate.

Prussia's primary concern was once again Poland, where a new government had tried to enact reforms and stabilize the country. The possibility of a renewed Polish-Lithuanian Commonwealth was unacceptable both to the Prussians and Russians. With Prussian forces tied up in France, Russia intervened in Poland. Of course, such actions alarmed Frederick William II, as it opened the possibility of Russian expansion and posed a threat to Prussia. Initially, he thought about supporting the Poles, but he found it much easier to find common ground with the Russians. After some discussion, by early 1793, the two nations had agreed to another partition of Poland. The Russians took almost half of the Polish territories in the east, some 97,000 square miles (250,000 square kilometers), while the Prussian crown was awarded 22,000 square miles (58,000 square kilometers) for not acting against them. The Habsburgs didn't react since they were too preoccupied with the French; in addition, part of their alliance with Frederick William stipulated support for further expansion in Poland. Thus, Prussia gained the cities of Danzig (Gdańsk) and Thorn (Toruń), which were important economic centers. Plus, it was more land than the king had even hoped for.

Merely a year after the Second Partition of Poland, the Poles rebelled against the stationed Russian troops and the Polish nobility loyal to Saint Petersburg. They were partly inspired by the French Revolution. This time, the Prussians were the first to act, yet their forces were stretched too thinly. The Russians and Austrians soon came to help, leaving the Poles without a chance. By late 1794, they had been crushed. The only thing that was left was for the three victorious nations to agree upon the third and final partition of Poland. Realizing that new territories would bring a further strain on the state administration and that the Prussian treasury and army were exhausted, Frederick William struck a peace treaty with the French in early 1795. Since Prussia was the first of the monarchies to yield to the French Republic, which was established after Valmy, it was seen as a betrayal and an act of cowardice from its former allies. Nevertheless, by October of that year, through negotiations with Russia and Austria, Prussia secured around 21,000 square miles (55,000 square kilometers) of Polish territories around Warsaw.

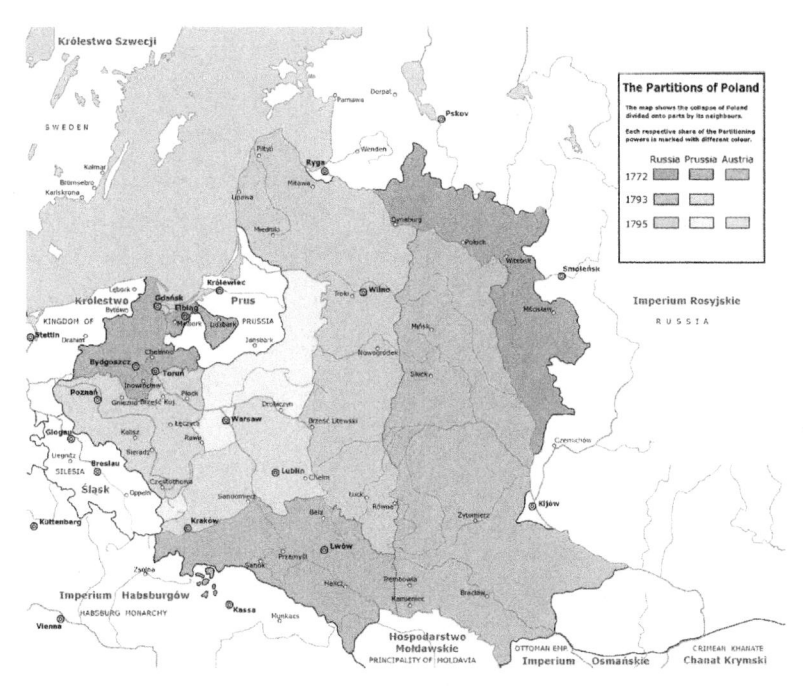

Map of the three partitions of Poland, with Prussian gains colored in blue.
Source: https://commons.wikimedia.org

However, from then on, Prussia was left isolated and alone. Frederick William II managed to ally and then abandon all the major European powers during his reign, making his messy duplicitous diplomacy unwelcomed in most courts. The Austrians released propaganda attacks, calling the Prussians cowards and wicked, with similar tones resonating with later historians. Yet, when looking at reality, for Prussia, it seemed like the best course of action. The new lands were rebellious, and the Prussian Army and administration were overextended and exhausted. Fighting against France, which, at the time, had shown little malice toward Prussia, seemed disruptive and unnecessary. The separate peace, at least on paper, also created a neutral zone in the northern Germanic lands and refocused the French on Prussia's traditional adversary: the Habsburgs. From that perspective, a separate peace seemed reasonable, yet its consequences showed that Frederick William lacked the foresight most of his predecessors had.

Besides being left without any allies and friends, Prussia's demeanor in dealing with France signaled that Berlin was apathetic toward the fate of the Holy Roman Empire, creating the final tear in its institutional fabric. In trying to preserve peace and increase his power, Frederick William II tried to influence other Germanic princes to follow suit. Soon, even the Habsburgs adopted such a stance, focusing on their own personal gains more than on the fate of the empire. An additional problem for Prussia was that with the destruction of Poland, it lost its only buffer state against the Russians in the east. Its future became intrinsically tied with its more powerful eastern neighbor. Nevertheless, for a short while, it seemed that Prussia might be well off. As one of the least impressive rulers in the Hohenzollern dynasty from the 16th century onward, Frederick William still managed to enlarge his state a third and increase the number of his subjects from 5.5 to 8.7 million. He passed away in late 1797 before he could see the full effects of his ill-advised diplomacy.

Frederick William II was succeeded by his son, twenty-seven-year-old Frederick William III. He was quite introverted and shy, and he was somewhat melancholic but also pious and honest. Like most of his Hohenzollern predecessors, he had a troubled relationship with his father. Frederick William III felt neglected by his father. He was raised by tutors and educators and thus suffered from an inferiority complex his entire life. The new king also felt disgusted by his father's court, which was filled with cliques and intrigues, as well as adultery. In contrast, Frederick William III was devoutly faithful to his wife, and he worked on restoring the morality of the Prussian court and cutting expenses. However, he also exhibited an unnatural distrust of his ministers and delegates. The young king wanted to personally dominate state affairs, but he lacked the capabilities of his great-uncle Frederick II. For this reason, his reign lacked consistency and efficiency.

Like his father, the new king was an average ruler who was thrown into one of the most chaotic periods of European history. Initially, Frederick William tried to remain neutral, staying out of the Second and Third coalition wars against France. In the process, he was willing to make territorial trades within the boundaries of the crumbling Holy Roman Empire, as did other princes and even the Habsburg Empire. In those dealings, Frederick William III relinquished some 1,000 square miles (2,600 square kilometers) and about 125,000 subjects in return for 5,000 square miles (13,000 square kilometers) and almost 500,000 people. Thus, the empire's number of constituent states dwindled while the Habsburgs continued their struggles against the French, who were slowly regressing into a monarchy under Napoleon Bonaparte. That tendency was confirmed in 1804 when Napoleon was proclaimed an emperor. This was coupled with the Habsburg emperor crowning himself as the "Emperor of Austria." After the War of the Third Coalition was over, the Holy Roman Empire was dissolved. In its place, Napoleon created the Confederation of the Rhine, an alliance of French client states that excluded both Prussia and Austria.

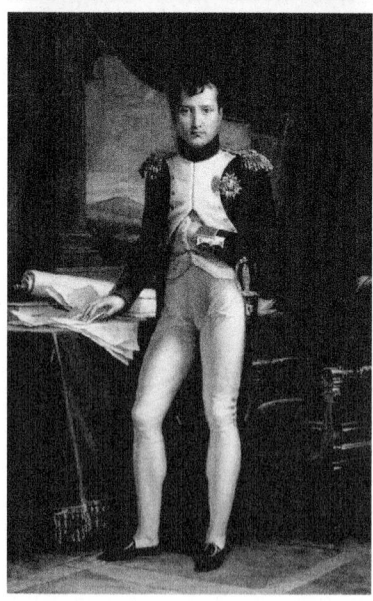

*Paintings of Frederick William III (top) and Napoleon Bonaparte (bottom).
Source: https://commons.wikimedia.org*

This was the final sign that Prussia wasn't going to be safe solely through the ink on paper. In the years that led up to the creation of the confederation, it became clear that, for the French, especially Napoleon, Prussia was merely a second-rate power. The supposed

Prussian domination over northern Germanic states that had existed due to a 1795 treaty was circumvented, as France did as it pleased. Its occupation of British-held Hanover in 1803 is probably the best example of this. Furthermore, not only was northern Germanic neutrality ignored but also Prussian noninvolvement. Both the Russian and the French armies crossed Prussian territory when they needed. By 1805, Frederick William III found himself in a precarious position. He needed to choose a side or be swallowed. He initially tried to ally himself with Russia and Austria in the Third War of the Coalition, but both empires yielded to France before he could join. Thus, Prussia had to realign with the French, becoming more of a client state than an equal partner.

When Napoleon created a new confederation in place of the Holy Roman Empire, he finally forced Frederick William to act. It excluded Prussia from the Germanic world while at the same time consolidating its client states and giving them higher titles. None of these actions were done with any consideration to the king of Prussia, which means he was dealt with like any other Germanic client prince. For the Prussians, it was all too much, even the pro-French in the court, prompting Frederick William to seek an alliance with Russia and Saxony. At the time, Sweden and Britain were already fighting France, making the bones of the Fourth Coalition, while the Austrians recovered from their previous defeat. Prussian involvement began with an ultimatum to Napoleon to withdraw behind the Rhine or face the consequences. It was sent on October 1st, 1806, giving the French a week to comply. This led to Prussia's declaration of war a day after the deadline since, as expected, Napoleon dismissed the ultimatum.

The French Army was already stationed in the southern Germanic states, so it marched quicker than the Prussians expected. Napoleon's army brushed through the initial Prussian defenses on its borders toward Bavaria as it marched to Berlin. By October 14th, 1806, the main Prussian forces met the French in a double Battle of Jena–Auerstedt in modern-day Thuringia. At Jena, the two sides had roughly equal troop numbers, around fifty thousand to fifty-five thousand men each. At Auerstedt, a similarly sized Prussian Army faced a French regiment that was twice as small. Despite that, both battles ended in a crushing Prussian defeat. The Prussian Army lost some forty thousand men, while many others surrendered. The entire military force built by Frederick William's predecessors during the 18th century had been swept away in a single blow. The royal court fled to East Prussia and the safety of Königsberg, while the rest of the kingdom was overrun by the end of the month. It was only then that the Russians managed to roll into the conflict from the east.

A later illustration of the retreating Prussian soldiers after Jena-Auerstedt. Source: https://commons.wikimedia.org

During the next several months, Frederick William and Napoleon tried to negotiate a peace treaty. However, Napoleon seemed hell-bent on humiliating the Prussians, despite showing immense respect to Frederick the Great while in occupied Berlin. All the while, the Prussians hoped that Imperial Russia could deliver a devastating blow to the French Army. In the end, despite some success, the Russian tsar lost the will to fight and agreed on peace negotiations in July of 1807. The two emperors met near Tilsit (modern-day Sovetsk) on a raft in the middle of the Niemen River, with Frederick William being left as an observer on the banks, only expanding on his humiliation. France and Russia concluded the Treaty of Tilsit, and Prussia had to accept the terms without negotiations. Napoleon reduced Prussia in half, both in size and population. Almost all the territories gained in the Second and Third Partitions of Poland were lost to a new Franco-Polish satellite state. At the same time, all Prussian possessions west of the Elbe River were given to French allies. Furthermore, Prussia had to pay an immense indemnity, some fifteen years' worth of its pre-1806 annual state revenue. The Prussian Army was reduced to merely forty-two thousand men. Finally, what was left of Prussia had to house and feed some 150,000 French occupation soldiers.

In the end, the Treaty of Tilsit finally reduced Prussia to the same level as all the other Germanic principalities, making it just another client state among many across Europe. The Hohenzollern monarchy hadn't found itself in such a position since the Thirty Years' War in the early 17th century, and it would leave a similar traumatic mark on the people's consciousness.

Chapter 7 – Recuperation through Reforms

With a single blow, Napoleon and the French had more or less set Prussia back almost a century, if not more. Its territory was reduced, its diplomatic position diminished, its military crippled, and its economy paralyzed. Prussia's very existence was threatened, as it seems the French emperor had only scorn for the Prussians. The Hohenzollern monarchy was spared because Napoleon wasn't sure what to do with it, while the Russians had advocated for its survival during the peace negotiations.

Before Frederick William III and the Prussian state stood two paths. One was to accept their fate and hope for a better tomorrow, or they could work on bettering their situation. The king and, more importantly, his closest advisors chose the latter, prompting a series of reforms in the next several years. Those changes were mainly led by Heinrich Friedrich Karl vom Stein and Karl August von Hardenberg, two experienced statesmen whose careers dated to the era of Frederick the Great. Their reforms are often represented merely as an answer to the Prussian state crisis after Tilsit; however, this debacle only gave impetus to changes that were slowly brewing behind the political scene. Their true roots were in the Prussian Enlightenment, which had been so wholeheartedly supported by Frederick II. During his long reign, the great Prussian king championed education, debate, free thoughts, and other expressions of culture. He worked hard on gathering some of the most notable thinkers in the Germanic lands and wider. It should suffice to say that one of the most famous philosophers of all time, Immanuel Kant, was one of many individuals who thrived in the fertile soils of the Prussian Enlightenment.

The Enlightenment, though, was somewhat stifled during Frederick William II's reign. He was more in line with traditional absolutism than his uncle's enlightened form. Nevertheless, many of the ideas and thoughts survived, and some even passed to his son, Frederick William III. His role is sometimes diminished in the reforms enacted by his bureaucrats, yet it was the monarch who gave them their position and the support needed to carry through with these much-needed changes. This was crucial, especially since most of the nobles seemed to be against any alterations to the existing system. Even more importantly, the king himself dabbled in reform ideas, inquiring about transforming the prison system and state finances before the defeat. He backed down partially because he found stern resistance among his officials but even more so due to his feeling of inadequacy. His lack of confidence was caused by the fact that his father didn't prepare him for the role of the monarch, although the king also had to contend with his shy personality. Nevertheless, this crushing defeat turned the atmosphere in the court around, and once again, Prussia was fertile ground for reforms.

Before delving into the details of Prussia's reforms, it is vital to note that they began under Stein's tutelage. He was the king's chancellor, but he became a thorn in Napoleon's side in late 1808, when French spies intercepted Stein's letter that was filled with anti-French sentiment. He pressured Frederick William to dismiss Stein, and for a while, the Prussian king resisted. Yet, in 1809, Stein fled into exile, and his work was continued by Hardenberg, with whom Stein worked closely while in office. Hardenberg not only continued but also expanded on Stein's ideas in the following years, though not always to Stein's approval. It is worth noting that these reforms were not solely Stein's and Hardenberg's fruits of labor. They worked with a number of scholars, economists, and statesmen to achieve all that they planned and wanted. Among them were Heinrich Theodor von Schön, Wilhelm von Humboldt, and Carl von Clausewitz, just to mention a few. In reality, the changes were brought about by the cooperation of a group of like-minded people under the king's service and support.

Paintings of Stein (top) and Hardenberg (bottom).
Source: https://commons.wikimedia.org

The reformers' first task was streamlining the government. Until that point, state bureaucracy was stuck in the old double-structured governance, with overlapping jurisdictions between the central and local administrations. The first order of business was to replace the old General Directory with the Ministry of State (*Staatsministerium*). It consisted of five ministers, whose authority no longer combined specified tasks and territories; instead, the ministers were given a single governmental field. Thus, there were ministries of the interior, foreign affairs, finance, war, and justice. The initial collegial nature of the Ministry of State was changed with the introduction of the state chancellor (*Staatskanzler*) in 1810, a position first awarded to Hardenberg. At a local level, Prussia finally created an integrated provincial system, abolishing the last traces of the historical ducal administration. Every province had its own local governmental body with a ministerial division similar to the central administration and a high commissioner (*Oberpräsident*), who was directly subordinate to and represented the Ministry of State. Provinces were administratively subdivided into districts and townships while also given locally elected diets to increase the idea of self-rule.

Such regional autonomy seemed to be one of the goals of the reformers, as Stein had also reorganized towns in a similar manner. He put all cities under the same administrative bureaucracy with identical rights and obligations. Then, he proceeded to return governing rights from the central to the local administration while also forcing the citizens to participate in them. In 1810, reformers also tried to uplift the idea of self-governance on a state level, as Hardenberg formed the Council of the State (*Staatsrat*), which was, in a way, the forerunner of the National Assembly. It was supposed to prevent the state from regressing into full absolutism, as the council would have a say on laws and administrative procedures. However, the council never managed to catch on, and Prussia remained without a parliament until 1848.

Frederick William wasn't merely a passive bystander when it came to the bureaucratization of the state. At some point, Stein wanted to curb the crown's authority by making a royal decree valid only if it had the signatures of all five ministers. Of course, the king refused, and Stein was, for a short while, in Frederick William's bad graces. Regardless, the new system unshackled the state from absolutism and its reliance on the capabilities of a single person and also made governing more efficient across the entire nation.

The second task set before the reformers was streamlining the economy, more precisely, state revenue. This was, in a way, the reformers' primary goal for these changes, as paying indemnity to France was the only thing keeping Prussia alive. Thus, Hardenberg worked on tax standardization, replacing a wide variety of local and minor taxes with statewide uniform taxation. Furthermore, excise taxes were expanded beyond just cities, though on a lesser variety of products, like luxury goods, alcohol, and tobacco. Taxation on the commercial and industrial sectors was also reorganized, with a progressively spread-out trade tax. New taxes were also added on income and wealth, but these were only marginally successful, as the nobility found a way to circumvent property taxes, leading to a class tax, an intermediate between the poll and income taxes. Apart from taxation, customs duties were also reformed, though this was finished only after Napoleon was defeated. Internal tariffs were lifted, as well as export bans set up by Frederick II. The import duties were heavier on products that competed with the local industrial economy, which was still too weak to fend for itself. Transport duties were also put in place, adding additional state revenue.

Overall, the reforms tried to spur the economy with more progressive taxation, with the intention to put the majority of the burden on the nobles and the rich. Such plans failed, most notably in the idea of equal taxation for all citizens, something the nobles protested. In that aspect, the reformers found themselves in a struggle with the fading aristocracy. However, for the nobility, the most troublesome issue was the termination of serfdom, which was carried out in the October Edict of 1807, followed by several more ordinances and edicts for further clarification and regulation. These included the problems of corvée labor, which had initially remained in place, as well as the issues of land ownership and reimbursement. Yet, the nobility quickly turned around and accepted the new system, as they realized they gained more through this new land distribution while the peasants gained little. Most of the peasants were unable to pay for their lands; thus, it would revert to the nobles, who would then hire the peasants as cheap labor. In the end, the agricultural reforms failed to make society equal, to some extent even furthering the concentration of wealth, but it did increase production output by modernizing the system.

The October Edict of 1807 (top) and Humboldt (bottom).
Source: https://commons.wikimedia.org

The more important byproduct of the abolition of serfdom was the peasants' freedom. After 1807, they were allowed to move and to do as they pleased with their lives, without being bound to the land or their masters. This allowed for a much-needed influx of laborers to the cities, giving a spark to Prussia's industrial economy. Luckily, the reformers were aware of the importance of industries. Thus, they enacted a policy of the freedom of industry, where the market dictated how it would develop. Guilds lost their monopolies, and their membership became voluntary. Anyone could set up an industrial workshop, wherever and however they pleased, as long as they acquired a state license. Furthermore, legal differences between the cities and the countryside in terms of industrial endeavors were eradicated. The basic principles of industry were now free competition and free professional choice. The only exception was mining, which remained a state monopoly until the 1860s. The liberalization of industry gave way to its rise, which, in turn, became the foundation of Prussia's economic rebirth.

An important part of the reforms was also the change in Prussian society. This was partially achieved by widening citizenship status. That designation wasn't limited solely to members of privileged township strata, as it also included all people who owned a house, including, in rare cases, single women. Thus, voting rights in cities were wider than ever before, though still limited to the local government levels. This was followed by the further inclusion of Jews in Prussian society. The Edict of Emancipation of 1812 gave them the same liberties, rights, and duties as all other citizens. However, Jews could still not achieve military ranks and high positions in the state administration. Of course, this was at least partially caused by economic necessity, as Jews had been previously banned from certain professions. However, this process was more a result of the Enlightenment, during which time Jewish society emerged out of isolation and came in contact with the Prussian elite. In fact, Hardenberg was a frequent guest in Jewish homes and counted many of them as his friends. Yet, full Jewish integration wasn't immediately achieved, as many Prussians held on to their misconceptions and prejudices against them.

Educational reforms were also part of the societal changes, and they were mostly headed by Humboldt. Like with the other reforms, the initial issue was the standardization of education. A wide variety of private, religious, and municipal educational institutions were molded into a three-tier schooling system, starting from People's Schools (*Volksschule*), the elementary level, after which came gymnasiums, which were then followed by universities. The main goal was to no longer merely teach specific subjects but instead turn children into people capable of learning for themselves. Humboldt then proceeded to open schools for teachers, helping the standardization of this system, which was completely under state control. Education was compulsory, and the state issued all curriculums and created exams. Furthermore, any civil service position required a certain level of education, and performance replaced one's social origin as the main qualifier. Apart from that, Humboldt's reforms also brought humanistic ideas to education, allowing schools to depart from the purely utilitarian form of the Enlightenment. He also envisioned the autonomy of universities and academia. The state and politics should be absent from them, leaving universities to pursue higher intellectual goals according to the scientific method. Thus, Humboldt's educational system, in theory, produced educated and interested citizens who were capable of self-governance.

Of course, there were others who deemed that, in certain areas, Humboldt was wrong. His humanistic individualism was often attacked the most. Many thought that education should be used to mold people for the needs of the state and, even more, the nation, especially as a form of resistance against Napoleon. However, in that aspect, military reforms were more important. Like other changes, these were done as a collaboration of several officers, with Clausewitz being probably the most famous of the group, even though he was the youngest. One of their principal complaints was that the Prussian

Army lacked motivation and that patriotism should be the main motivator for soldiers. In turn, service in the army should instill nationalistic feelings in the soldiers, creating a loop, as these thoughts would then be passed to their sons and neighbors. This was only furthered by reorganizing the army to treat its soldiers better, more like people than simple objects. The most severe physical punishments were abolished, and additional loyalty was also created by opening officer ranks to the non-nobility and basing promotions more on merit than on one's background.

Apart from rekindling the people's morale, the army went through important restructuring, similar to the governmental organization, making it much more streamlined. Additionally, the Ministry of War acted as a precursor to the Chief of Staff, and the army modernized both its equipment and training, creating more mobile and flexible units. The existing officer corps was purged, and tactics were updated. Finally, compulsory universal conscription was enacted, making all grown male adults viable for service if needed. This replaced the old system, which had been degraded even during Frederick II's reign into a bunch of foreign mercenaries serving the Prussian crown. Furthermore, a system of local militia was set up in 1813, creating the first seeds of the later *Landwehr*. It was supposed to be used solely for defending Prussian soil, and it wasn't part of the regular army, but later reforms would change that. The military reformers also found a way to train new soldiers while abiding by the Treaty of Tilsit. They rotated them so that there were never more than forty-two thousand active soldiers at a time.

Overall, the entire state was preparing to stand up to Napoleon. The military changes were aimed at equalizing the odds on the battlefield, the economic reforms gave strength to the home front while also buying time by paying the indemnity, and the new administration made it all better organized. Least of all, reforms brought a new sense of unity and patriotic feelings to the Prussians. Despite that, Frederick William III was cautious about provoking the

French. While the reforms were still ongoing, there were several mentions of rebellions and rejoining the war against Napoleon, yet the king decided not to act. Many in his court urged him to do something since the humiliating feeling of being under France's boot only accumulated. Nevertheless, Frederick William was aware that if Prussia stood up too soon, it might perish. Thus, years passed while resentment grew. It culminated in 1812 when Napoleon forced Berlin into a military treaty against Russia. Prussia was to open up its forts and quarter the French Grand Army (La Grande Armée) on its way east, as well as add twelve thousand Prussian soldiers to the cause. For some, like Clausewitz, that was too much, and a number of military officers defected to the Russian tsar, where they met up with the already exiled Stein.

Quartering some 300,000 men of the Grand Army rekindled the memory of the Thirty Years' War and the destruction caused by foreign armies. It also showcased that even the new Prussian system wasn't able to effectively house and feed such a mass. Nevertheless, the Prussian king stood silently. Rebellious emotions flared when the first news of French defeats near Moscow reached Prussia, yet Frederick William was still unsure if he should act. During December 1812, he remained inactive, but his subordinates began deciding instead of him. First, Clausewitz managed to persuade the Prussian part of the Grand Army to join the Russian cause and cease to assist the French retreat. Throughout January, the Prussian government slowly distanced itself from France, and the king fled from Berlin. Then, in early February 1813, Stein entered East Prussia, which basically ceased to heed Berlin and prepared for war against Napoleon. The spirit of insurrection spread across the remainder of Prussian lands, and in late February, Frederick William finally decided to side with the Russian Empire. In early March, he declared war and called upon his people for support in the struggle.

Early spring was mostly spent on preparations by both sides, with the first major combat occurring in May. These ended in French tactical victories, but they were paid for in a large number of casualties on both sides. A short armistice was agreed upon in June, allowing for some respite. By that time, Britain, Sweden, and Austria decided to officially join the new coalition. The latter two contributed armies, while Britain gave much-needed monetary subsidies. In August, the armistice ended, and hostilities resumed. Napoleon managed to gather more than 400,000 men, but many lacked proper training. Against them stood a coalition army of some 500,000 soldiers, around half of which were Prussians. The military reforms allowed Prussia to enlist 6 percent of its total population, meaning it had the largest army amongst the allies, despite its predicaments. It's vital to mention this was only the German front, as the Napoleonic Wars were fought across Europe and the world. Once the fighting resumed, battles were fought with mixed results. Several minor coalition victories were annulled by a single major French victory. Nevertheless, the Grand Army was slowly losing its footing, and Napoleon needed a decisive triumph.

He was unable to separate the allied army to defeat it, slowly maneuvering into a dead-end. The French were unable to retreat anymore, and Napoleon decided to accept a full-on battle at Leipzig. The two sides clashed in what amounted to be the largest battle of the war. It became known as the Battle of the Nations, with some 600,000 soldiers coming from France, various Germanic states (including Prussia), Russia, Sweden, Austria and all of its Hungarian and Balkan territories, Poland, and Italy. There was even a single British brigade present. At the height of the clash, the French had some 225,000 men against some 380,000 coalition soldiers, leaving them at a disadvantage. Nevertheless, the battle lasted from October 16th to October 19th, 1813, but it concluded with a decisive French defeat. Napoleon lost some seventy-three thousand men, while the coalition had some fifty-four thousand casualties, out of which sixteen thousand were Prussians. In the end, the Grand Army was forced to retreat to

France, while most of Napoleon's Germanic allies abandoned him. His armies and supporters on other fronts were also losing, yet he refused a generous peace treaty sent by the allies, most notably the Austrians, who wanted to preserve a strong France as a balance to Russia.

A painting of the Battle of Leipzig. Source: https://commons.wikimedia.org

By late 1813 and early 1814, the coalition forces had entered France. Napoleon managed to achieve some smaller victories, but he no longer had an army capable of full-on resistance to numerically superior allies. The war ended in April 1814 when the French Senate deposed him. The deposed emperor was exiled, and the Bourbons were restored in Paris. By the autumn of 1814, the major powers, including defeated France, gathered at the Congress of Vienna to resolve the territorial and political issues left by the wars. However, in March 1815, Napoleon managed to return to France and gathered some loyal veterans in an attempt to win his throne back. Impressively, he gathered more than 250,000 soldiers, but he faced three to four times as many allied forces. In the end, Napoleon's final defeat came at Waterloo, Belgium. His 70,000 men stood against some 170,000 allied soldiers. Here, a crucial role was played by the fifty thousand Prussians under General Gebhard Leberecht von Blücher, who saved the British from collapsing and allowed the Duke of Wellington to turn the battle around. For that, Blücher was awarded an honorary doctorate from Oxford. In the end, Napoleon was defeated once and for all, and the Prussians proved their mettle as they slowly rebuilt their military reputation.

While the last coalition dealt with Napoleon's attempt of resurgence, the Congress of Vienna continued. It gathered some two hundred diplomats and statesmen of all European nations, including representatives of Bourbon France. However, the future of Europe was more or less forged by five major powers: Britain, Russia, Austria, Prussia, and France, despite its defeat. For Prussia, which was represented by Hardenberg and Humboldt, it was recognition. However, the Congress of Vienna showed that the other major powers didn't fully consider Prussia to be an equal member. Its representatives didn't acquire the gains as they were instructed, instead depending on agreements of other powers. Their main goal was to annex Saxony; however, the politics of the greater powers interfered. Prussia was given some 60 percent of its territory back; instead of receiving the rest, it gained the Duchy of Posen in Poland to block Russian expansion. The rest of the Polish territories gained in the Second and Third Partitions of Poland were willingly ceded to Russia even before the congress. Prussia also regained its western part, while Britain advocated for its further expansion in the Rhineland in an attempt to control France in the future.

The Prussian diplomacy defeat was even more pronounced when the question of the Germanic future arose. Prussia advocated a strong, dually centralized entity under a shared Austro-Prussian hegemony; in a way, it would be a reformed Holy Roman Empire in accordance with new levels of power and influence. However, Austria wanted a loosely tied union of free states, with a singular centralized body that was nothing more than a constant assembly of diplomatic representatives. In the end, the Austrian plan won, and the German Confederation was created. It encompassed thirty-eight Germanic states, though not all the Austrian and Prussian territories were part of it. For the latter, Posen and West and East Prussia remained outside of the confederation. Nevertheless, even in the newly formed confederation, there was a clear sense of dualism between Berlin and Vienna.

In the end, despite nearing something of a diplomatic failure at the Congress of Vienna, Prussia was left on solid ground. It had acquired significant territories, and the Hohenzollerns, for the first time, held more Germanic lands than their traditional Habsburgian foes. Their old competition was destined to flare once again.

Chapter 8 – Expanding Dominion over the Germanic World

The French Revolution and the subsequent Napoleonic Wars sent shockwaves across Europe. Entire political and social systems were uprooted across the continent. After a rather turbulent decade, Prussia, returning once again from the brink of destruction, found itself with something of a fresh start.

In geopolitical terms, it seems that Prussia's main preoccupation was ensuring its supremacy in the German Confederation, which essentially was a substitute for Prussia's previous disregard of the Holy Roman Empire. This subsequently made Austria its main political opponent. Its ministers focused mostly on two major questions: the joint security of the Germanic states and economic cooperation. The latter was done through the creation of the German Customs Union (*Zollverein*) in 1834, which incorporated almost all the Germanic states except for Austria. The whole process was slow, and Prussian politicians weren't initially in favor of such plans. It only began actualizing in 1827 when Prussia arranged for a customs agreement with Hesse, then slowly lured, blackmailed, or forced the rest of the states into the union. It was an important step toward dominance, yet it proved too shallow, as no real loyalty was achieved. Furthermore, even the economic gain from it remained largely limited.

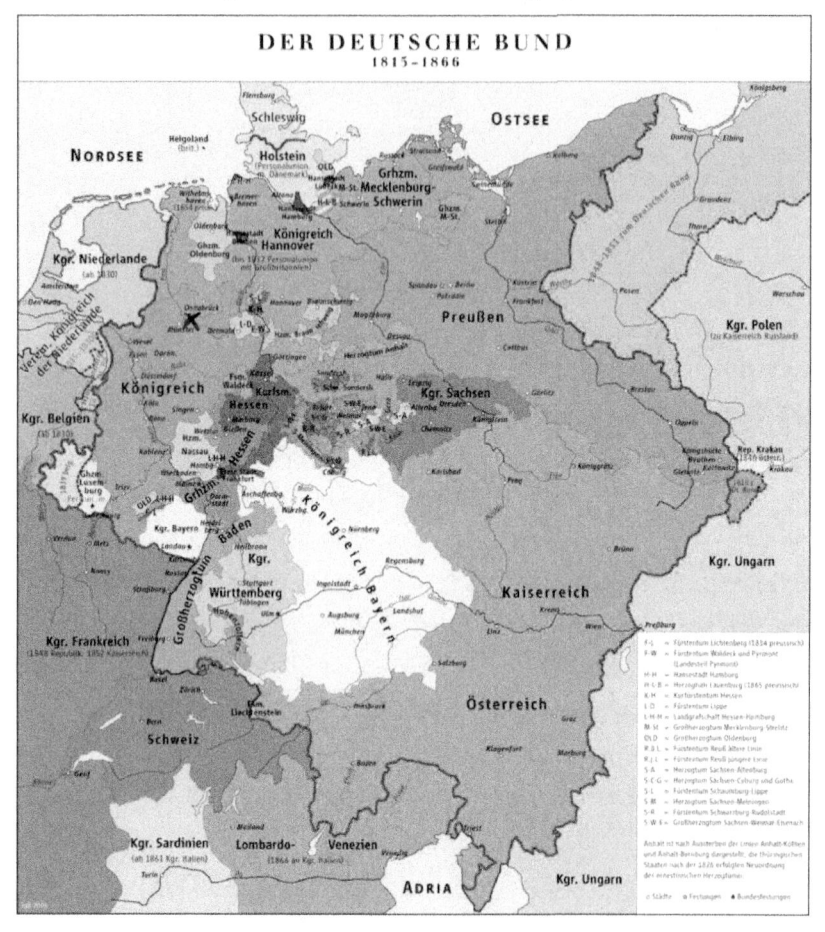

A map of the German Confederation, with Prussia colored in blue (lighter blue are territories outside of the confederation).
Source: https://commons.wikimedia.org

The federal security issue was essentially an attempt to create a unified Germanic army that would defend all the states. The Prussians tried to create such an organization both in 1818, when Napoleon's occupation was still an open sore, as well as in 1830, when France went through another revolution, deposing one branch of the Bourbons for another. In both instances, the foreign threat was seen as the lesser of two evils. The question of a joint military was reheated in 1840 when a new French government demanded reinstating France's borders on the Rhine. The issue was resolved peacefully, as neither side was really looking to start another war, but a more direct threat faced the German Confederation: its weakness. Its response was to create a string of federal fortresses, mostly toward France, as well as adding steps toward integration of the different Germanic armies. However, these never managed to lead to a proper fighting force, as bureaucracy and diplomacy made it quite inefficient and slow.

In the end, neither the Customs Union nor the Federal Army brought Prussia closer to dominating the Germanic lands. It was still necessary to maintain decent relations with Austria and to even cooperate with them at certain points, like, for example, agreeing to a military union in the case of a French attack during the 1840 Rhine Crisis. Nevertheless, such actions did bring Prussia some respect, especially as it almost always seemed more progressive and liberal than Austria. Yet, most states remained wary of Berlin's pretensions, at least the governments.

The common people's nationalistic ideas of a unified German people began to arise, mostly as a response to Napoleon's occupation and subsequent French nationalistic outbursts. Since Prussia bore the brunt of the fight against the French, it also gained slightly more attraction in such circles as well. This is especially evident in the 1813 campaign, which became known as the War of Liberation, indicating its "Pan-Germanic" character. However, during Frederick William III's reign, these outbursts of German nationalism were rare, as nationalism itself was only in its infancy, far from the political and ideological driving force it would become.

In internal affairs, Prussia was facing its own dualism. On the one hand, because of the supposedly "dangerous" fallout of the French Revolution, there was a growing conservative political wing. Its representatives worked hard, mostly against any kind of populist groups, as well as progressive politicians aiming at transforming Prussia into a parliamentary monarchy. These forces prevailed in the end, with many progressives losing their posts, Humboldt being one of them. The liberal dream of a national assembly was stifled for a while. Furthermore, conservatives reduced the local diets into more of an advisory body than proper political representation. The liberal vision was not achieved, at least partially thanks to the internal squabbles between liberals but also because Frederick William III sought to appease the Russians, who were still leaning heavily toward absolutism. The Prussian king even married off one of his daughters to the Russian tsar, allowing for these connections to be even tighter for a while.

Regardless of that, the progressive spirit remained. This was most notable in the education system, which remained among the best in the world, with some 80 percent of children attending. It continued to produce citizens who could at least read, but in many cases, they could do even more than that. That played in hand with the growing economy and industrialization that was picking up pace. Not only did it allow for more professional workers, but the state also opened institutes for technology, importing the knowledge and technology that were needed to kickstart the Prussian industrial revolution. Such modernization was eased by the fact that the Rhineland territories were already quite urban and were considerably rich in coal. The Ruhr region was notable for that kind of natural riches. Thus, the economy was also growing toward a progressive industrial future, but it should be noted it wasn't yet booming. Major improvements came in the late 1830s with the first railways, which connected Berlin and Potsdam. This new transportation technology would soon expand across the kingdom.

Another aspect of Frederick William III's later reign was achieving some kind of bureaucratic and national unity. After 1815, Prussia gained various new territories and had to incorporate new systems and nationalities into the state. These were achieved in various ways, but it proved especially difficult with the new Polish subjects in Posen. They were among the few non-Germanic nations within Prussia, and they were certainly the largest non-German-speaking minority. On top of that, they never came to terms with losing their homeland. To some extent, they and other minorities went through the Germanization process but never completely or too aggressively. Additionally, more urban western provinces were a stronghold of progressive civic ideas, somewhat counterbalancing the more conservative eastern lands.

Another disbalance could be found in the laws. While the state worked on once again equalizing the whole system, the results varied. Some new provinces completely adopted the Prussian system, some adopted parts of it, and some acknowledged it merely on paper. In that regard, probably the most notable difference was that the Edict of Emancipation remained active only in the "old" Prussian lands, making only parts of Prussia open to Jews. Apart from that, Frederick William III also tried to unify all the Protestant denominations in Prussia under the so-called Union of Evangelical Churches. It was meant to unify both the Lutherans and Calvinists without changing their religious practices and beliefs. Despite that, the religious unification didn't go too smoothly, as it included some coercive measures, as well as local schisms.

In the end, Frederick William III ended his reign peacefully in June 1840. His rule was marked by great turmoil, somewhat distorting our image of his capabilities, but he managed to keep Prussia afloat. Regardless of that, it was clear that, with his rule, the ideas of a strong and independent Hohenzollern monarch came to an end. He was the first king whose reign was heavily dependent on his ministers and whose power was no longer fully absolute. He was succeeded by his eldest son, who became known as King Frederick William IV. The new king was well educated in various fields, but he never showed any special talents, except in drawing. Since his childhood days, he seemed more of a daydreamer; thus, he grew into an avid romanticist. Additionally, Frederick William IV was a deeply religious and pious person. All of that combined to form a person in love with the romanticized image of medieval Germany, which dictated his policies throughout his reign.

That kind of idealized vision of politics and the monarchy make Frederick William IV hard to categorize. He dangled between the liberals and conservatives, leaning to one or another from issue to issue. On the one hand, he championed more liberal politics, such as reduced censorship and tolerance toward religious schismatics and the Poles. The new king also made local diets convene more regularly and rehabilitated some earlier reformers who had fallen into disfavor. Yet, in contrast, he refused to accept ideas of a constitution or national assembly and also retained some sense of a conservative stance toward social class issues.

However, this doesn't mean that Frederick William actually agreed with either side; rather, he wanted to create some sort of reconciliation between the two political forces in hopes of restoring the Prussian subjects' faith in the monarchy and rekindling some sort of medieval feudal loyalty. Some of his romanticized views came from his religiousness, as he saw the kingship as a divine right, giving him a holy insight into the needs of his subjects. Such politics went against liberal constitutional-parliamentary ideas, but they also didn't appeal to the conservative circles since it seemed he wanted to recreate the medieval state. To almost everyone in government, it seemed as if he was ignoring reality.

A photograph of Frederick William IV from 1847.
Source: https://commons.wikimedia.org

Despite his political anachronism, Frederick William displayed impressive economic progressiveness. Since his youth, he had favored the idea of transforming Prussia from an agricultural to an industrial state, supporting the import of foreign technology and expertise. To aid in that kind of development, the king and the state supported infrastructural expansion, with the most notable being the railway system. Unlike his predecessor, Frederick William IV not only gave his wholehearted support for railway expansion, but it was also his preferred mode of transportation. Thus, during his reign, the Prussian textile industry, coal mining, and mechanical engineering picked up speed. These industries were concentrated in Ruhr and Silesia, which were traditional manufacturing centers, as well as around Berlin. Industrial and economic output slowly grew, adding an overall positive effect on the state's wealth. However, it simultaneously created a new set of social issues, as the new urban working class began showing signs of discontent with the political system, as well as their working and living conditions. Thus, Prussia was constantly plagued by minor worker revolts and strikes, with the most famous being the Silesian Weavers' Revolt of 1844, during which Frederick William IV was the target of a failed assassination attempt from a disgruntled former civil servant.

A painting of the developing industry near Berlin.
Source: https://commons.wikimedia.org

The king's response to the issue was once again somewhat paradoxical. He personally donated money to associations of the working class. Yet, at the same time, he issued the General Prussian Industrial Code of 1845, which banned strikes, making them punishable by imprisonment. It seems that Frederick William felt compassion for his subjects, as he never tried to suppress their revolts too harshly, but he wanted to keep the "third class" from rising and disrupting the social balance. However, he failed to recognize that the balance had already been disrupted. During the 1840s, there was a noticeable process of pauperization of the lower classes, followed by occasional food shortages. These issues proved to be the most common motivators of protests, which notably remained local in nature. Some scholars tried to connect the issues with the Malthusian idea of population outgrowing the food supply, yet it wasn't true. Much like industry, agriculture was also developing due to new technologies, like artificial fertilizers, which significantly increased food production. Nevertheless, those advances didn't make agriculture resistant to natural and biological misfortunes, which caused short-term shortages. The more apparent reason should be found in the high number of people moving to the cities looking for jobs, which made unskilled labor quite cheap.

Apart from that, it should be noted that the noble class was also slowly losing ground. For decades, starting from the Napoleonic Wars, aristocrats were slowly losing their estates, a trend noticeable in Europe as a whole. By the 1850s, in certain areas of Prussia, they held only some 50 percent of their lands from the beginning of the 19th century. With that, the nobility was slowly losing its material influence in favor of the "new rich," the industrials and merchants. Nevertheless, the aristocracy kept a strong influence on politics, and the two upper classes often managed to find common interests. The final aspect of the changing social and political scene was the evolution toward so-called "popular politics." As the masses became more literate, newspapers and pamphlets fueled political debates. These were often illustrated with various caricatures, adding a visual aspect while making the message easier to understand. Songs and smaller theatrical pieces at carnivals were also popular media for political agitation and expression. Overall, it was the ongoing politicization of popular culture, making politics part of everyday life. More importantly, it also began reaching much wider corners of society, meaning it was no longer limited to the higher classes.

Amidst such changes, Frederick William IV wanted to expand the railway network to directly connect Brandenburg with the Rhine provinces. This was partially caused by economic necessity but even more by the need for military transport and a stronger political connection. However, such an investment required sizable funds, prompting the government to search for a loan. The only problem was that a law from Hardenberg's time prevented the state from raising credit without the approval of a national assembly. It was, in essence, a combination of all the provincial diets into a single body, and it was tasked only with approving the state loan. On the surface, it seemed like a law to prevent the state from spiraling into debt, but it was, in fact, left as a future tool to put pressure on the king to engage in liberal reforms. Despite that, Frederick William downplayed the possible complication and convened the United Diet in April 1847. It immediately became a controversial issue, as liberals saw it as a possible political platform. Nevertheless, the king warned them in the opening speech that there was no earthly power that could force him to sever his divine monarchical ties with his subjects for a sheet of paper, a metaphor for a constitution.

Unfortunately for him and his conservative supporters, the warning went unheard. Liberals of all kinds came together and acted in unison, blocking the loan. They demanded that the United Diet be transformed into a proper legislative body. In contrast, their conservative opponents were unable to work cohesively since their politics championed provincial autonomy, leaving them merely on a defensive footing. In June, the diet was adjourned without approving the loan. It was an anticlimactic end, but it signaled that social unrest was growing and that the Prussian people wanted to finally put an end to the absolute monarchy by creating a constitution and a parliament. It was a powder keg waiting to explode. The government felt that pressure, especially the king, who became a primary target of caricatures and political attacks. In response, censorship was somewhat tightened, as well as police control and scrutiny. The state reverted to engaging in political and social oppression.

The social storm was brewing, but it wasn't limited only to Prussia or the Germanic states. People across Europe were beginning to voice their displeasure with the dominant conservativism, demanding more liberal and democratic politics. Uprisings, revolts, and revolutions began spreading across the continent, starting with Switzerland in late 1847 and the Italian states in early 1848. However, proper revolutionary zeal began to catch on only after the February 1848 Revolution in France. It was fueled by nationalist and republican ideals, which quickly caught on in the already socially unstable Prussia, as well as other states of the German Confederation. The first major protest in Berlin began in early March. Clashes between demonstrators and police ensued, leaving some casualties. The court was unsure how to proceed. Some hawkish elements, including the king's younger brother, Prince Wilhelm (William), wanted the military to stifle the revolt. Others were in favor of a milder stance or even a compromise. It was only after the fall of the conservative government in Vienna that Frederick William decided to buckle and avoid further confrontations. Instead of fighting the revolution, he would lead it.

Rioting in the streets of Berlin in 1848.
Source: https://commons.wikimedia.org

On March 18th, the public gathered in front of Frederick William's palace, where he tried to publicly proclaim the convening of the United Diet and the drafting of the constitution. However, the presence of armed troops caused panic amongst the protesters, and due to this confusion, a massive clash between the protesters and guards ensued. Once again, Frederick William decided to de-escalate the situation. Instead of unleashing the army on the protesters, he withdrew it from the city while staying himself. This appalled many, as it was seen as the subjects infringing upon the monarch's rights. It even prompted the short exile of Prince Wilhelm, who expressed his utmost displeasure with the act. Nevertheless, the king stood his ground and allowed the formation of a national assembly tasked with drafting the constitution. However, once given the power, protestors fractured. There were various liberal and democratic ideals at play, but most importantly, there was a strong radical wing that was leaning toward what we could say Marxist ideas. Their presence pushed many toward the liberal center, lessening the assembly's revolutionary spirit.

A wood engraving of a session of the United Diet.
Source: https://commons.wikimedia.org

All the while, Frederick William negotiated with the representatives about the constitution, but it was hard to find common ground. Then, in late November, unsatisfied with the overall development of the changes, the assembly called for a tax strike. For the king, it was a step too far, so he enacted martial law and dispersed the protestors. By then, revolutionary zeal was largely gone, and it proved to be an easy and quick victory for the government. The United Diet was officially dissolved on December 5th, but Frederick William followed that by issuing his own constitution that was an agreeable middle ground to gather support from most of the liberals and moderate conservatives. Additionally, such a political approach alienated the more radical elements on both sides of the political spectrum, which allowed Frederick William to begin his work on restoring Prussia's social unity.

However, democratic and liberal ideas were only one aspect of the European Revolutions of 1848. The other major aspect was nationalism. In the Germanic states, it posed a question of the unification of the German people into a single state. The main proponent of such ideas was the Frankfurt National Assembly, the first elected parliament of the German Confederation. Ultimately, its main goal was to formulate how and on what basis Germany should reunite into a single state. The assembly began its work in May 1848, with the main issue being if Austria should be accepted into the new state and in what scope. There was also the question of if the state should have a king and if the post should be elective or hereditary. Ideas of a republic were also brought in. While the other Germanic states were still struggling with their own internal revolutions, Frederick William IV had already accepted, though cautiously, the idea of unification. He said that Prussia would become a part of Germany, all the while carrying an armband of the German national colors: red, black, and gold (or yellow). In essence, the idea of restoring the German Empire was in accordance with his romantic interpretation of history, but the Prussian king seemed reluctant that it was the "proper" way to do it.

A drawing of Frederick William IV riding through Berlin after supporting the goal of German unity. Source: https://commons.wikimedia.org

Even before the Frankfurt National Assembly convened, Prussia and Frederick William accepted the role as the protectors of the German realm. In early 1848, they clashed with the Kingdom of Denmark over the future of the Schleswig and Holstein provinces. Those territories were ruled under a personal union of the Danish king while still being part of the German Confederation as separate entities. Pressured by inheritance issues and a wave of nationalism, the Danish king tried to annex and integrate the two provinces into Denmark. That move outraged the local German population, as well as the rest of the confederation. In response, Prussia sent a part of its army to Schleswig and Holstein in April of that year. It had the

German Confederation's official endorsement, and the Prussians quickly pushed the Danish defenders back to Jutland. The other major powers were quick to react to this move, though. Most notably, Britain and Russia warned Frederick William he was going too far, asking for a withdrawal and a peaceful mediation.

This left Prussia in a tight spot, strung between the Frankfurt National Assembly and the threat of a much greater confrontation. In the end, Frederick William buckled and signed a treaty with Denmark in August 1848. However, part of the German Federal Army, which had gathered by then, continued the struggle, claiming they were under the jurisdiction of the assembly, not the Prussian king. The separate peace was seen as Frederick William's betrayal of German nationalism since he had acted on his own accord.

Nevertheless, the Frankfurt National Assembly was still grateful for the assistance of Prussian troops in suppressing violent radical revolts in Baden. Overall, though not successfully, Prussia acted as a guardian of the German Confederation. Thus, when the Frankfurt National Assembly finally reached its conclusion, it decided to create a nation-state without Austria, as it had too much of a non-German population. By March 1849, it sent an official offer of the imperial crown to Frederick William. Surprisingly, he rejected the offer. It was not that he didn't dream of being a German emperor, but rather, it was because the way the assembly attempted to do it was wrong in his eyes. First, he wanted Austria to be kept a part of it. Secondly, he felt that a national diet didn't have the right to offer him anything; only the institution of the old medieval elector princes could. Frederick William replied that the assembly could ask him to be an emperor but that it didn't have the right to offer him a crown.

That rejection brought the Frankfurt National Assembly to an end. It was a clear defeat of the nationalistic ideas of unification, at least for a while. Yet, at the same time, it showcased that Prussia had become the most influential Germanic state. For the first time in history, it overshadowed Austria.

Chapter 9 – Final Evolution into the German Empire

Refusing the imperial crown from the national assembly may have ended revolutionary ideas for the unification of the German realm, but it wasn't the last attempt. Despite what might have seemed a defeat of nationalism, the desire for a united Germany remained strong.

The next attempt at fulfilling the German dream came from Frederick William IV. After refusing to be crowned emperor, he began working to form the so-called Erfurt Union. This was a federation with other Germanic states, excluding Austria, based on arrangements with their rulers. The other monarchs expressed some initial interest in this, laying ground to its formal existence in mid-1849. However, it never received much public support, and hammering exact agreements among more than twenty sovereign rulers proved to be an impossible task. Another issue was Austria's stance. Initially, Vienna showed signs of interest, as it was proposed that the Erfurt Union would, in turn, be loosely tied with Austria in a broader coalition or confederacy. Yet, by late 1849, the Habsburgs turned aggressively against it, seemingly when the other Germanic states began showing their doubts, with some even leaving the federation. Instead, they began advocating the resurrection of the, by then, defunct German Confederation.

By early 1850, Berlin and Vienna were staring at a possible conflict. While Prussia continued with its attempts to realize the Erfurt Union, Austria partook in the revival of the old confederation. The final straw came in autumn when the ruler of Hesse-Kassel asked for the German Confederation's military aid. Since that land was straddled between Prussian territory, it led to further friction, alarming Frederick William enough to order full mobilization. However, Austria was backed by the Russian Empire, making an open war impossible to win, which forced Prussia to back down. In late November 1850, the two Germanic states signed the so-called Punctation of Olmütz, forcing Prussia back into the confederation with a promise of some reforms. Another point that was also added was that the Schleswig-Holstein issue would be dealt with by the German Confederation as a whole, as the First Schleswig War was still ongoing, though without direct Prussian interference. The end result of the Olmütz treaty was yet another diplomatic humiliation for Prussia, as it restored the German Confederations in 1851 with almost no changes, and there was also the final conclusion of peace with Denmark in 1852 under the tutelage of all major European powers. Schleswig and Holstein remained under Danish rule but with some constitutional limitations.

For many in Prussia, the Punctation of Olmütz was another humiliation, showing that most major powers still looked down on it. Yet, Frederick William had more pressing matters to deal with. Though the revolution was stopped, there were still some smoldering remnants, especially in the Rhineland region. Most of the protests were led by the more radical leftists, who were influenced by Karl Marx, and the king knew their ideas had to be suppressed. Apart from that, the state needed to be reformed to follow the new constitution. Putting down rebellions in the western provinces proved relatively easy, as the radicals never had wide support. Reforming the state proved a bit more difficult since the system needed some fine-tuning. The Landtag of Prussia (*Preußischer Landtag*, the Prussian parliament) was formed, and it was divided into two chambers. The upper consisted solely of the nobility, similar to the British House of Lords. Initially, its representatives were supposed to be at least partially elected, but by 1853, members were only appointed by the king. The lower house was the House of Representatives, whose members were elected.

However, the voting was based on the three-class suffrage system. That meant the voters were divided into three voting classes based on their income, with all electing an equal number of representatives. This meant that the wealthiest 4.7 percent of the population had the same voting power as the 12.7 percent of the second class and the 82.6 percent of the third class. Thus, the new system favored the rich and nobles. Additionally, under the new constitution, ministers answered only to the king, who kept all his executive powers and retained the power of the judicial veto. The monarch also retained supreme command of the army and the right to sign treaties and declare wars. Finally, the sovereign wielded the right to amend the constitution, which Frederick William IV did several times up until 1857. Apart from the central government, local governments and the legal framework were tuned for the new system, once again aiming at the equalization and functionality of the state. The final change was the addition of new taxes, although old taxes were also reformed. This increased the state's revenue, which, in turn, allowed the government to increase its investments and speed up the development of the economy, most notably industry.

All the while, Prussia remained largely inactive and neutral in diplomatic matters. Thus, when the other European powers went to war against Russia in the Crimean War (1854-1856), it remained on the sidelines. However, it marked the break between the Russo-Austrian alliance, which would prove to be vital for Prussia. Similarly, Berlin remained neutral when the Italian War of 1859 erupted. This was a conflict between the Habsburgs and the Kingdom of Sardinia, which was backed by France and sought Italian unification. The Prussian Army was mobilized to secure its western frontiers, but its alliance negotiations with Vienna failed. In the end, the Italo-French alliance won, creating fertile ground for the proclamation of the Kingdom of Italy in 1861.

The war showcased several important international factors. First, nationalistic ideals were still strong, and the unification of Italy reheated the question of a German nation-state. Secondly, it exhibited the loss of Austrian power while, at the same time, boosting the reputation of the new French Empire. The latter had become an imperial monarchy in 1852 after a coup, and it was ruled by Emperor Napoleon III, Napoleon's nephew. Finally, it emphasized the relative weakness of Prussia through its inactivity, prompting some observers to question its status as a major power.

This irked Prince Wilhelm, who became regent in place of his brother in 1857. Frederick William IV had suffered a series of strokes, rendering him almost speechless and mentally impaired. Since he had no children, he willingly gave power to his younger brother. At the time, Wilhelm was sixty years old, and he was militarily oriented and a former staunch conservative who quickly adapted to the new system. Thus, from his perspective, the only way to acquire recognition and political influence was through a strong army. He began leaning toward such developments at the start of the regency, but he really picked up the pace after his brother's death in 1861. Once he became King Wilhelm I, he immediately pushed for the renewal of military strength, which had not been significantly improved since 1806; in fact, it had somewhat deteriorated. The liberal-led assembly tried to block Wilhelm by refusing to fund it, which prompted him to install Otto von Bismarck as his prime minister. Bismarck, who was a crafty politician, managed to outplay the liberals. Together with Minister of War Albrecht von Roon and

Chief of Staff Helmuth von Moltke, a famous field marshal, they began reforming the army.

An 1857 photo of Wilhelm I (top) and an 1860s illustration of Bismarck, Roon, and Moltke in said order (bottom). Source: https://commons.wikimedia.org

Moltke's idea was to increase the number of active soldiers, adopt new types of arms, master quicker and better mobilization, improve communication and deployment using modern technologies, and create a more professional and well-trained officer corps. While the field marshal worked on these, Bismarck worked on securing his political position and began forging the path to the ultimate goal of his government: the unification of Germany. The first real test came in 1863 when the Schleswig-Holstein situation flared up once again. A new Danish king had tried to merge Schleswig with Denmark, breaching the 1852 treaty. Of course, the German Confederation immediately reacted. In late 1863, a small Federal contingent entered Holstein before Austria and Prussia jointly declared war against Denmark in January of the following year. It was a relatively short war, lasting only a few months. A German victory was almost certain from the beginning since the Danes received no international backing due to their breach of an international treaty. It ended in August of 1864, with both provinces officially ceded to the German Confederation under the direct and shared control of Austria and Prussia.

The war and victory showcased two important things. One was that the Prussian military reforms were moving in the right direction. Its achievements were really spectacular, especially in comparison with the Austrians. The second thing the war illustrated was that military leadership functioned better when it was under the primacy of political leadership. Bismarck was the conductor of all activities, even though his stance angered some of the generals. All the while, elderly Wilhelm I was slowly relinquishing the reins of the state to the prime minister, though not without his influence. What ensued was often depicted as Bismarck's grand scheme of some sort, yet in reality, he just proved to be an adaptive and cunning politician. The situation at Schleswig and Holstein remained unresolved, to a degree on porpoise, creating increasing tensions between Austria and Prussia.

While the hostilities were slowly heating up, Bismarck went on to create fertile diplomatic ground for a confrontation with the Habsburgs. First, he secured an alliance with the Kingdom of Italy since parts of Italy were still under Austrian control. Then, he secured Russian neutrality, which was easily achieved, for Saint Petersburg was still hostile toward Vienna. Britain was already uninterested in German affairs, which means the final nail in the coffin was France. Bismarck ensured Paris wouldn't intervene, giving a vague unwritten promise to Napoleon III that he could expand in Belgium and Luxemburg in return.

By the summer of 1866, Austria and Prussia were on the brink of war. Both sides began a series of local and partial mobilizations. Austria tried to unanimously convene the local Holstein diet, which gave Bismarck an excuse to send troops to occupy it on the basis of Austria's infringement of the joint sovereignty. In response, Vienna turned to the Federal Assembly. Most members of the German Confederation condemned the invasion and voted in favor of their mobilization against Prussia. The Prussian representative eventually walked out on the assembly, stating that, for Berlin, the German Confederation was dissolved. The war began on June 14th, with Italy joining five days later. On the Prussian side stood a number of smaller Germanic states, with most of the large ones, like Bavaria, Saxony, and Hanover, siding with Austria. At the start of the war, most observers expected an Austrian victory, as they still considered the Prussian forces to be the underdog. However, Moltke and his reforms were quick to prove them wrong.

While the majority of Prussian forces began their offensive in Bohemia (the modern-day Czech Republic), its secondary troops dealt with the Hanoverian troops, as they were an immediate threat to Prussia's rear. Then, according to Moltke's grand plan, the main Prussian Army in Bohemia sought a quick and decisive battle. Somewhat unwillingly, the Austrians met the invading forces at the Battle of Königgrätz (present-day Sadová) on July 3rd, 1866. There, despite their ineffective artillery, Prussia's superior training, officer leadership, and innovative infantry rifles won the day against the Austrians. Although the Prussians were marginally outnumbered, they managed to inflict around twenty-two thousand casualties and as many captured on the Austrian army. While the main force continued to advance through the Czech Republic and Slovakia, other Prussian troops defeated the Saxon and Bavarian troops. The Austrians, knowing they were facing total defeat, asked for peace on July 22nd, ending the war in a mere seven weeks.

A painting of the Battle of Königgrätz. Source: https://commons.wikimedia.org

Bismarck was keen on accepting the peace without prolonging the war. He was concerned major powers might choose to intervene, and the economic factor was also a concern. Furthermore, the prime minister wanted to avoid too much revanchism from Austria or other Germanic states. The peace was ratified in Prague in late August, but not without French interference. Prussia annexed Schleswig, Holstein, Hanover, Hesse-Kassel, Nassau, and Frankfurt, while the rest of the northern Germanic states were organized into the North German Confederation. Prussia basically controlled the confederation's military and foreign relations; in other words, these states were basically just a step away from annexation.

The ultimate result of the war was Austria's exclusion from German affairs, most notably the question of unification. The only way forward from there was a union without Austria or any other Habsburgian lands—a union referred to as Lesser Germany

(*Kleindeutschland*). The victory of 1866 also cemented Bismarck's government, though he still faced staunch opposition, and nationalistic fervor began boiling over. It was only a matter of time before Prussia made the final step toward a German nation-state.

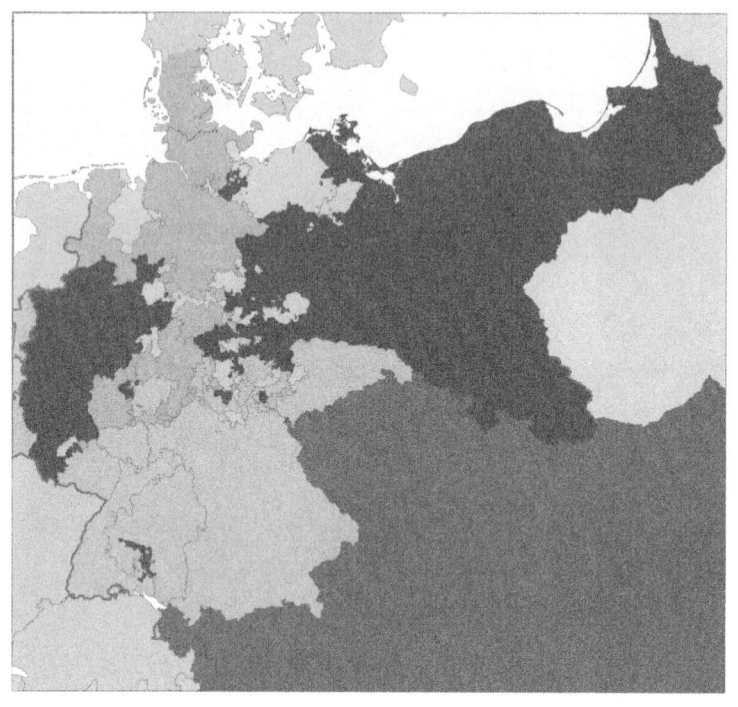

Map of the Austro-Prussian War of 1866—Austrian Empire (red), Austrian allies (pink), Prussian allies (light blue), Prussia (dark blue), Prussia acquisitions (cyan), and neutral states (green).
Source: https://commons.wikimedia.org

Initially, Bismarck thought it might be possible to achieve a peaceful unification, but the southern Germanic states remained quite suspicious of Prussia. He tried to alleviate this problem in 1868 by forming an all-German Customs Parliament (*Zollparlament*), which would strengthen Prussian ties with the southern Germanic states. However, the attempt was ultimately a failure. By then, Bismarck realized that what Prussia needed was an external enemy that would bring the entire German nation together. France fit this role perfectly. Emperor Napoleon III had remained unsatisfied after the Austro-Prussian War. Instead of leaving the German realm fractured and weakened as Napoleon had hoped, France stared at an enlarged and strengthened Prussia. In 1867, Napoleon tried to buy Luxembourg, but Bismarck pulled diplomatic strings to prevent that from happening. This went against their spoken agreement, and it stirred up resentment against Franco-Prussian relations.

Once again, many historians frame the upcoming series of events, starting with the Luxembourg crisis, as part of Bismarck's "grand design." However, once again, he merely proved his political skills and flexibility to utilize opportunities the best he could. Even the Customs Parliament played a double role; apart from trying to sway the southern states, it was also aimed at irking the French, as it was another step toward unification. From Napoleon's perspective, a united Germany was the last thing France could afford since it posed all kinds of threats, not to mention thwarting his plans. Bismarck was aware of that when he continued to build on the tensions between Paris and Berlin, all the while handling internal political struggles with both the liberals and more radical conservatives. In the background, Moltke was finalizing his reforms, introducing a new artillery piece to resolve the issues from the Austro-Prussian War while also leaning into better training, expanding the army, and utilizing new technologies, like railways and the telegraph.

Continuing to masterfully play both German and French nationalistic feelings and constantly pouring oil onto the fire, Bismarck used every opportunity to provoke Napoleon into declaring war. For his plans to work, Prussia had to be in a defensive position. Among many smaller incitements, a particularly fertile one started in late 1869 when the Spanish Parliament offered a crown to Wilhelm's cousin. Initially, every member of the Hohenzollern family was against it, but Bismarck plotted for the cousin to accept. While he was working on that, he caused a few smaller provocations, but to no avail. Then, in the spring of 1870, he finally persuaded Wilhelm's cousin to accept the throne, causing an immediate reaction in Paris. It seemed all was going according to plan, but then Wilhelm I intervened and put a stop to the Spanish affair. Bismarck was crushed, and he almost gave up before the French made a crucial mistake. Their ambassador tried to gain further promises and public statements from the Prussian king. It was too much for Wilhelm, who simply refused. He sent notice to Bismarck about the conversation, which the prime minister used to create a modified version in which the talk seemed more abrupt and impolite, a move that aimed to stir the fiery nationalists on both sides. The message, the so-called Ems Dispatch, was circulated across European newspapers, including in France.

For Paris, this insult was the cherry on top, and they declared war on July 19th, 1870. Bismarck's plan had finally worked. The southern Germanic states immediately joined Prussia, both because of their existing agreements but also because of nationalistic fervor. The idea of yet another Napoleon ravaging the German realm was unacceptable for most. The rest of Europe was decidedly neutral in the conflict. On the one hand, Napoleon didn't have any more allies nor sympathies, while Bismarck was already on friendly terms with Russia and Italy. Austria was still recovering, and Britain seemed to be at terms with Prussian-led Germany. Nevertheless, all the observers expected a longer war and slightly favored the French, as its military was still considered to be among the best in the world. However, from the onset, it was clear that the Prussian military reforms were paying off. They mobilized the army faster and produced more soldiers, even though Prussia had fewer citizens. Then came the first serious clashes in early August, most notably Spicheren and Froeschwiller Woerth, which all ended in Prussian victories.

A 1910 painting depicting the Prussian infantry during the Franco-Prussian War. Source: https://commons.wikimedia.org

The Prussian Army advanced through France in three columns, taking a series of victories against the passive French defenders. By mid-August, the main French fighting force was besieged in Metz, which consisted of their best troops. Napoleon III gathered what remained of the French military and attempted to relieve Metz, but he was forced away from it, so he headed to the fortress of Sedan. Once there, he was forced into a battle against the numerically superior Prussian Army and its allies. Napoleon was defeated and captured, along with the entire army. Soon afterward, Metz surrendered as well, and the rest of the Prussian forces moved to besiege Paris. The French imperial regime crumbled, giving way to yet another republic.

Despite that, France was determined to fight. The people's nationalism was too strong. The new government in Paris tried to relieve some pressure by organizing new armies, but those ad hoc regiments were no match against the well-trained Prussians. Thus, on January 26th, an armistice was signed, officially ending the hostilities on January 28th, 1871. The entire war lasted roughly six months and proved to be nothing more than a pure demonstration of Prussian power. France seemed like a third-rate state compared to it, something that completely shocked Europe.

To put it in perspective, the combined Prusso-German forces had some 140,000 casualties and captured soldiers. The entire French Army had 140,000 dead and as many wounded, while an additional 750,000 were captured. Such a conclusive victory finally proved the worth of Moltke's reforms, as the basis of the Prussian victory lay in enlarging the army through universal conscription, ensuring better-trained soldiers and officer cadre, and using new communication and transportation technologies. And all of this was topped off with aggressive strategies and mission-based tactics, allowing for a more flexible army. However, the military remained under the government's reins, something of which Bismarck continuously reminded the military leaders, which caused some friction.

While the war was still ongoing, Bismarck began negotiating with the southern Germanic states about joining the new confederation. When they accepted, the Prussian prime minister proposed going a step further and restoring the German Empire. Thanks to his political machinations, which included bribery, he managed to gather enough votes in the Federal Assembly to proclaim the formation of the German Empire (*Deutsches Kaiserreich*) on January 18th, 1871, in Versailles. It was a political double entendre, as it humiliated France and marked the anniversary of the Hohenzollerns' formal inauguration as the kings in Prussia, which happened in 1701.

A later rendition of the proclamation of the German Empire at Versailles.
Source: https://commons.wikimedia.org

The unification was thus finalized. The Prussian king now became German Emperor Wilhelm I while still holding onto his title of king. This was only further formalized when the French were forced to recognize the empire in their peace treaty, with Bismarck going on to further humiliate them. He annexed Alsace and Lorraine, border territories near Germany, which were also industrial centers of France. Additionally, he forced a huge indemnity on the losers. It was, in a way, payback for what Napoleon had done to Prussia and the rest of Germany, especially when considering that the German occupation of northern France wasn't handled lightly. Thus, Prussia, now transformed into the German Empire, managed to fulfill its long-lasting dream of uniting the German people and cementing its position as a major world power. An additional bonus was that its lightning-fast victories also created a myth of German military superiority, which often stretched back to the time of Frederick the Great. At least for a while, Prussia's and Germany's future seemed bright.

Epilogue

The newly formed German Empire used the constitution of the North German Confederation as its basis. Thus, formally speaking, it was a tighter federal union of twenty-six entities, one of them being the Kingdom of Prussia. With that in mind, it could be said that Prussia "survived" the unification, as did the other Germanic states. However, from 1871 onward, its history became more of a part of German history than an individual story. Regardless, it should be noted that due to its central role in German unification, as well as the fact that the Hohenzollern dynasty ruled the empire, Germany was very much based on Prussian culture, traditions, and politics. Other states were slowly remodeled to fit the Prussian state system. This wasn't a significant change in most cases, as many Germanic states were already following the successful Prussian system, and their economies had also been interlinked for decades.

Over the next roughly forty years, the German Empire continued to grow and develop as a state. Most notable was the industrial boom, which placed it in the top three world economies. Politically speaking, it continued to swing between the conservatives and liberals, and the Prussian cultural model remained the most prominent. Emperor Wilhelm I continued his reign until 1888, and he was succeeded by his son, Frederick III, who ruled for a short time before his own son took over. Under Emperor Wilhelm II, Bismarck finally lost his place as the imperial chancellor in 1890. With that, the once-content German Empire set its sights on bigger goals, joining the colonial race while also trying to expand its influence. The combination of nationalistic and power politics pushed it toward a confrontation with the other major powers. The long-lasting tensions finally erupted with World War I in 1914, when Germany and Austria fought against Russia, Britain, and France. In 1918, Germany was defeated, with the empire being dissolved. The Hohenzollerns were forced to abdicate.

Nevertheless, Prussia as an entity survived as a "free state" or one of the constituent republics of the German Weimar Republic. The new government considered breaking up Prussia into smaller states, as it comprised roughly 60 percent of German territories, but conservative elements preserved it in its entirety. During the 1920s and even more so during the 1930s, a new wave of modern nationalism swept Europe and Germany, leading to the rise of the Nazi Party and Adolf Hitler. The new regime had a love-hate relationship with Prussia. On the one hand, they glorified its past, most notably Frederick II and its role in Germany's unification, and also adopted its militaristic and cultural heritage. On the other hand, they weren't fond of some of its traditional and conservative ideas. Thus, by the start of World War II, Nazi propaganda highjacked Prussian history and mythos, warping it to fit their perspective of the world. Their propaganda was so powerful that when the Third Reich was defeated, the Allies saw the Nazis as merely the latest example of "militant Prussianism." This finally led to the end of Prussia. Its territories were divided up, with large chunks remaining outside of German borders, while the rest was renamed to fit their pre-Prussian names. Thus, the region around Berlin became known as Brandenburg once again, bringing the tale of Prussia full circle.

Conclusion

The history of Prussia is a tale of ups and downs, destruction and revival, a tale of constant change and reforms in pursuit of survival and power. It showed a small and inconsequential Germanic state beating all odds and traversing the dangerous and destructive labyrinth of history to become one of the mightiest nations in the world. At some points, its fate dwindled on the edge, depending solely on the stubbornness of its leaders. At other times, it managed to take great strides forward, fueled by the genius and foresight of its rulers. In that aspect, its history depicts all the greatness that can be achieved through hard work and a bit of luck. Nevertheless, it is also a reminder that no nation is too big to fail and that no idea is too pure to be tainted. A great power that needed roughly three centuries to rise to its full power was toppled in mere decades, taking its ideals with it. As such, it is also a cautionary tale, reminding us that staying humble when achieving greatness is a virtue. Finally, it is a story of the interconnectedness of hubris and humility that entwines human lives.

Hopefully, this short guide gave you a basic idea of how Prussian history developed over the centuries, showing you that simplifications of it being just "good" or "bad" isn't how we should judge countries, nations, and people. History, as well as present life, is rarely that simple. It is a thought that is always worth remembering when judging both individuals and groups. Another important moral of Prussia's story is that constant change and adaptiveness make a difference, as one should recognize one's chances and take them. In the end, all of these lessons are what makes history worth reading and understanding. It teaches us about our present and our lives and helps us understand each other and the larger picture in which we live.

Here's another book by Captivating History that you might like

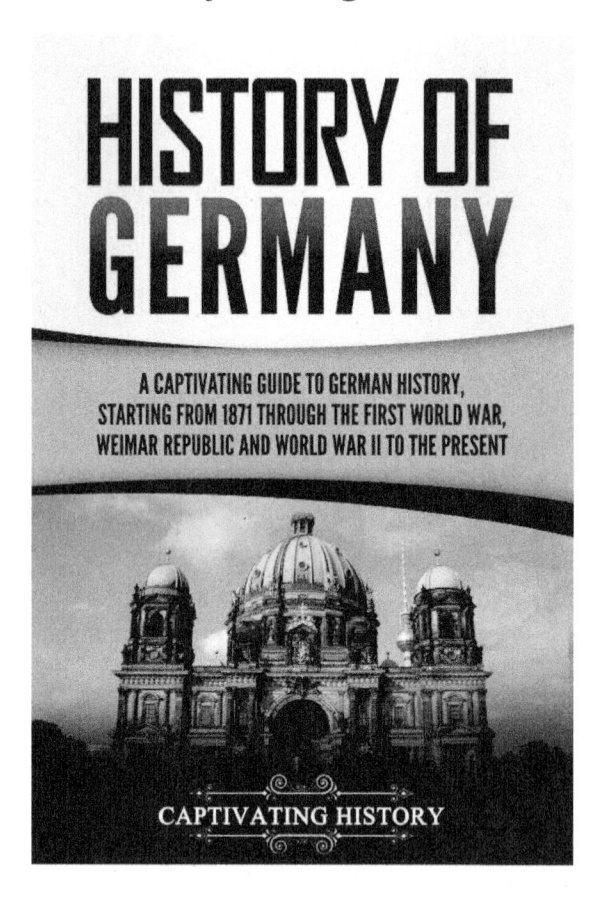

HISTORY OF GERMANY

A CAPTIVATING GUIDE TO GERMAN HISTORY, STARTING FROM 1871 THROUGH THE FIRST WORLD WAR, WEIMAR REPUBLIC AND WORLD WAR II TO THE PRESENT

CAPTIVATING HISTORY

Free Bonus from Captivating History (Available for a Limited time)

Hi History Lovers!

Now you have a chance to join our exclusive history list so you can get your first history ebook for free as well as discounts and a potential to get more history books for free! Simply visit the link below to join.

Captivatinghistory.com/ebook

Also, make sure to follow us on Facebook, Twitter and Youtube by searching for Captivating History.

Bibliography

Christopher Clarck, *Iron Kingdom - Rise and Downfall of Prussia 1600-1947*, Penguin Books, 2007.

Martin Kitchen, *A History of Modern Germany, 1800-2000*, Blackwell Publishing, 2006.

John G. Gagliardo, *Germany under the Old Regime, 1600-1790*, Routledge, 2013.

Joachim Whaley, *Germany and the Holy Roman Empire Vol. 1 &2*, Oxford University Press, 2012.

Margaret Shennan, *The Rise of Brandenburg-Prussia*, Routledge, 1995.

Mary Fulbrook, *A Concise History of Germany*, Cambridge University Press, 1991.

S.A. Eddie, *Freedom's Price - Serfdom, Subjection, and Reform in Prussia, 1648-1848*, Oxford University Press, 2013.

Philip G. Dwyer, *The Rise of Prussia: Rethinking Prussian History, 1700-1830*, Routledge, 2013.

David Blackbourn, *The Long Nineteenth Century - A History of Germany, 1780-1914*, Oxford University Press, 1998.

Jason Philip Coy, *A Brief History of Germany*, Facts on File, 2011.

A, Farmer and A. Stiles, *The Unification of Germany 1815-1919*, Hodder Education, 2007.

Peter Wende, *A History of Germany*, Palgrave Macmillan, 2005.

Jonathan Steinberg, *Bismarck: A Life*, Oxford University Press, 2011.

Stefan Berger, *A Companion to Nineteenth-Century Europe 1789-1914*, Blackwell Publishing, 2006.

Dennis Showalter, *The Wars of German Unification*, Bloomsbury academic, 2015.

Otto Pflanze, *Bismarck and the Development of Germany – The Period of Unification 1815-1871*, Princeton University Press, 1963.

Donald S. Detwiler, *Germany - A Short History*, Southern Illinois University Press, 1989.

Printed in Great Britain
by Amazon